THE WALKING
Shoes

FINDING THE RIGHT FIT

*Many hills will be climbed, and mountaintops reached in our lifetime.
It will often be as we walk in the valleys that we learn the true
Meaning of perseverance and find the perfect fit.*

JUANITA VIANELLE

1ST EDITION EDITED BY JESSICA SPRINGGAY FRANTZICH
2ND EDITION EDITED BY RHONA T. LEE

The Walking Shoes
Finding the Right Fit
1st Edition Edited by Jessica Springgay Frantzich
2nd Edition Edited by Rhona T. Lee

This book is written to provide information and motivation to readers. Its purpose is not to render any type of psychological, legal, or professional advice of any kind. The content is the sole opinion and expression of the author, and not necessarily that of the publisher.

All verses taken from New International Version and and New Living Translation Bibles unless otherwise noted.

Copyright © 2023 by Juanita Vianelle.

All rights reserved. No part of this book may be reproduced, transmitted, or distributed in any form by any means, including, but not limited to, recording, photocopying, or taking screenshots of parts of the book, without prior written permission from the author or the publisher. Brief quotations for noncommercial purposes, such as book reviews, permitted by Fair Use of the U.S. Copyright Law, are allowed without written permissions, as long as such quotations do not cause damage to the book's commercial value. For permissions, write to the publisher, whose address is stated below.

Printed in the United States of America.

ISBN   978-1-64552-160-0   (Paperback)
ISBN   978-1-64552-161-7   (Digital)

Lettra Press books may be ordered through booksellers or by contacting:

Lettra Press LLC
30 N Gould St. Suite 4753
Sheridan, WY 82801
1 307-200-3414 | info@lettrapress.com
www.lettrapress.com

TABLE OF CONTENTS

Dedication v
God's Easel vii
Introduction ix

PART I: SEASON OF ABIDING 1

Chapter 1   We're All a Work In Progress 1
Chapter 2   God Knows Where We Are Headed 3

PART II: SEASON OF PRUNING 31

Chapter 3   I Found What I Was Looking For 31
Chapter 4   The Rag 32
Chapter 5   Resting In His Arms 39
Chapter 6   Give Them Wings 40
Chapter 7   Love 43
Chapter 8   He Understands 44
Chapter 9   Our Reward 46
Chapter 10 Serenity 48
Chapter 11 Relationships 51
Chapter 12 Why the Children 56
Chapter 13 A True Friend 61
Chapter 14 So Little Time 65
Chapter 15 In His Time 69
Chapter 16 When We Get To Heaven 72
Chapter 17 Through Alexandra's Eyes 76

Part III: Season of Questioning 79

Chapter 18 What's Wrong With Common Sense? 79
Chapter 19 Is God An Unloving God? 84
Chapter 20 It's Just Stuff 87

Part IV: Season of Frustration 91

Chapter 21 God's Pause Button 91
Chapter 22 Innocence of a Child 93
Chapter 23 Lord of All 95
Chapter 24 Looking For La-la 96
Chapter 25 He Knows Our Thoughts 98
Chapter 26 A Mystery and No Clues 101

Epilogue 107
Recipe for Smiles 109
About the Author 113

DEDICATION

Blessed is the man who perseveres under trial,
because he has stood the test,
he will receive the crown of life that
God has promised to those who love Him.
-—James 1:12

To my husband David, a shining example of perseverance.

To my godmother Beth Lothringer, whose encouragement made this book possible.

To Jan Strech, my adopted mom who always has a shoulder to lean on.

To the kids and parents in the Enchanted Playhouse. Thanks for the memories.

To my friends who meet at my kitchen table for a weekly Bible Study. An oasis, a refuge from the stress and struggles of everyday life. We stand with open arms to provide spiritual support, comfort in sorrow, and a place of belonging. We have stood side-by-side learning the true meaning of perseverance: running forward with the goal in sight; to never hang our head and feel sorry for ourselves; to learn values and set boundaries; to always find something to be thankful; to find serenity by leaning on Jesus Christ; to trust God's plan even when we don't understand.

God works in mysterious ways and often with a sense of humor. When feelings of lameness overpowered my purpose and desire to continue writing, Jessica Springgay Frantzich reentered my life after many years. Jessica was one of the kids in my Enchanted Playhouse, who for ten years played a part in teaching me to laugh, to hug, to love, to like who I am.

GOD'S EASEL

I stand quietly and watch as a blanket of fog slowly covers the bay outside my bedroom window. A seagull lands on a nearby smokestack. The engines from passing tugboats join together to play a calming lullaby, while flashing red lights guide their way through still waters. Distant barking of seals coming through the chilled night air is accompanied by the tuba notes of a lighthouse foghorn.

I pull the curtain across my bedroom window, now separating myself from God's serene masterpiece of darkness, which seems to be whispering, "Goodnight." Moments later, my eyes remain closed and I listen to the stormy wind tossing waves and rain pounding the deck outside my room. I'm not alone. I know that only God can orchestrate such a performance. I lay snuggled under my blankets and I dream.

I awaken to sunlight creeping into the corners of my room. I open the curtain, take a deep breath, and begin the new day God has painted for me.

The men were amazed and asked, "What kind of man is this?
Even the winds and the waves obey Him!"
--Matthew 8:27

I form the light and create darkness, I bring prosperity:
I, the Lord, do all these things.
--Isaiah 45:7

INTRODUCTION

*All around Him was a glowing halo,
like a rainbow shining through
the clouds. This was the way the glory of the
Lord appeared to me.
When I saw it, I fell face down in the dust, and
I heard someone's voice speaking to me.
----Ezekiel 1:28*

    One of my favorite sites is rainbows pouring into the sanctuary of the old Community Church, through a stained-glass window on sunny mornings. The tiny church has few remaining pews, since many of the churches in Bend use their sanctuaries as multipurpose rooms and folding chairs are the norm. There is nothing wrong with this arrangement, although I would prefer holding church services outside under a tree to having basketball hoops hanging over my head. Sitting in the back pew, which is my family's favorite spot to sit in any church, and without basketball hoops, I sometimes feel drenched in a prism of pastel colors.

    Pastor gave a great sermon and one that took little concentration to keep up with. Good thing, since I stared at a single hiking boot with a cuffed sock attached throughout most of the morning. It laid on the floor to the side of the pew where I sat. Pastor spoke on the Trinity and how there is no way to prove it. "Just assume it's true and accept it," he said. He added that there is nothing in the Bible to prove the words came from God. "Just assume it's true and accept it, he said. But I heard"—Don't be scared and don't work so hard. Believe as a child and spend the rest of your life basking in God's sunshine enjoying His rainbows."

In the meantime, I couldn't take my eyes off that rainbow-colored drawing on the floor and the image in my mind of Jesus holding a paintbrush and smiling. By the end of the sermon the sun had cast another rainbow of colors to form a picture of a second boot instep behind the first. "Does anyone else see this?" I wondered. I read through Footprints in the Sand in my head, in which God walks with us and never leaves us. Could this have something to do with what I saw on the floor?

As I gazed upon the image next to me, I thanked God for allowing me to be a child, His child. I thanked Him for showing me those beautiful rainbow-colored hiking boots this morning. These imaginary shoes, appearing so real I could reach out and touch them, told me God walked around in sandals for a long-time telling people to believe in Him. The world and its people have become thicker skinned and harder to reach. These shoes told me God will go to any measure to bring us to Him, even if it means trading His comfortable sandals for a pair of rugged hiking boots, taking Him to the roughest terrain to rescue us. These shoes reminded me that God never turns His back on us.

No one will avoid tough times in this world. Some may get by with only a scratch while others, for reasons we may never know, don't completely heal from the storms that hit. I haven't written to pound any one over the head with my personal knowledge of Christ. It's not my intent to judge or attack another's faith or religion either. This story was written by me and for me but sharing it, I believe is God's will. Learning that I'm not responsible for another's salvation is one of the most helpful lessons I've mastered. My hope is that my story may set an individual on a new avenue of thinking and gaining a new perspective on life. Turning them, not by force, in the direction they truly want to go.

There is a pair of shoes for everyone, but first we must put aside our human emotions and walk by faith. We must put away our pain and disappointment and walk consistently everyday trading ragged edges in our lives for smooth surfaces only Christ can offer. Which pair of walking shoes will you choose for an incredible journey? ***Dear friends do not be surprised by the painful trials you are suffering, as though something strange were happening to you. But rejoice that you participate in the sufferings of Christ, so that you may be overjoyed when His glory is revealed. –1 Peter 4:12-13***

After nine rugged years of climbing from valleys up to mountain tops, I am learning that while it feels good to sit, our learning is done by climbing. While walking four-legged companion, Sissy, a sixteen-year-old dachshund, I thought of another title for this story. It is one all too familiar to many of us: *"I'd Ask God If I Wasn't So Tired!"*

During a Bible study on the book of Ruth, I felt a smile on my face when I had no answer for the second question on the homework assignment sheet. The first question had read, "What makes you bitter and the ink had spilled out on the paper with ease. Question two had asked, "How will you handle your bitterness now or in the future?"

I had written so much to answer the first question that I had to turn the paper over. Now, sitting in class, I saw I had forgotten to write an answer for question two. And it was OK. God had changed my heart and had taken away a considerable amount of bitterness. We all have a purpose to fulfill in this life, and we may not fully know what that purpose is until we are sitting at the feet of Jesus. By then, though, we may forget to ask. If, by sharing my story just one person comes to trust our Heavenly Father will bring them through their troubles and know that He is always near, I may be fulfilling the purpose in life God has chosen for me.

No matter what life has in store, we must never lock God out of our lives. No matter how difficult it is to believe in Him while going through trials and hardships we must believe. No matter how ugly the world gets we need to engrain in our hearts that God loves us and will protect us. God will turn each painful situation into a blessing if we surrender to Him.

PART 1

Season of Abiding

We're All a Work In Progress

Let the word of Christ dwell in you richly as you teach and admonish one another with all wisdom, and as you sing psalms, hymns and spiritual songs with gratitude in your hearts to God.
--Colossians 3:16

Looking back over time I realize we're all a work in progress and some of us may have more work to be done in us than others. First day in a Bible class, in a Bend church I attended while on a pilgrimage to escape from what seemed to be daily disasters, was a doozy. My comment, when told God wants us to forgive and pray for our enemies, still brings a laugh to those who were there. "Who me?" Forgive and pray for people who ruined my life? Forgiving family is one thing, but to pray for people outside my family who hurt me seems impossible, unless I pray they look into a mirror every day and remember what they did. And how will I know if I've forgiven them unless they are standing in front of my vehicle with the motor racing and me behind the wheel?"

A year later I dreamed about my enemies. I woke up unafraid and with no trace of anxiety. Another time I went to bed and was praying when I heard the words "Forgive my enemies." I must have laid there in the dark saying these words over and over in my head while wondering where that came from. I knew the answer. I told God, "They are yours now. I don't want them any longer."

Sometimes it is much easier to lash out and try to get even with those who hurt us. I am slowly learning that God uses even our enemies to give us strength and enrich our lives, if we allow Him room to work in us. It will take time to rid myself fully of the resentment been stored up. It helps to remember something written in a Dear Abby column years ago, "Resentment is letting someone live rent-free in your head."

Webster's Dictionary defines dream as: "A series of thoughts, images, and feelings which come to a person during sleep." In the dictionary I find no mention of who sends them. Fascinating is the word I use each time I see one of my dreams coming to life. I was not sent a dream to prepare me for what was to come when my husband and I planned our retirement. Odd that I never thought to look up a definition for retirement until typing it just now. Isolation, loneliness, withdrawn are the words used in the dictionary to define retirement.

A prudent person sees danger and takes refuge, but the simple keep going and suffer for it. --- Proverbs 22:3. A feeling of embarrassment and heartbreak overshadow my emotions as I read the definitions of prudence and simple. My dictionary defines prudence as: "Good judgment and foresight of the future." Simple is defined as: "Free from complexity, naive, unsuspecting." My story deals with my husband and I being simple and placing our trust in mankind. Here's the definition of trust: "Committing yourself to another's honesty, confidence and assurance."

A wooden plaque, a gift from my husband when we were first married reads, *Blessed Are Those Who Expect Nothing For They Shall Not Be Disappointed.* I lived my life according to those words on the plaque until retirement and then learned I should have had them branded into my brain.

"Most people complain the Bible is filled with too many do's and don'ts, so they go through life without reading it," a California pastor once said. "They wonder why everything is a struggle with so many questions going unanswered." I went to Sunday school and I flipped through pages finding verses, but I never read the Bible. Once I did, I found the Bible is the best "How-To" guide for living you will ever read. We must remember though; God gave each of us a brain and a heart and I'm pretty sure He doesn't mean for them to sit idle. We are to use them to show how glorious He is and maybe how glorious we can be in His image.

God Knows Where We Are Headed

*How much better to get wisdom than gold,
to choose understanding rather than silver!
---Proverbs 16:16*

I once received a daily devotional explaining how we sometimes make the mistake of believing that the most powerful Christians are the ones who sail over life's problems. Those people have great stories that they tell repeatedly about how God delivered them from something in their distant pasts. This kind of "ministry" is not really helpful, because, in reality, no one sails over everything. We only think they do. So those people with their "perfect" lives only perpetuate a myth that, in the long run, isn't helpful to anybody.

There was no way to avoid the pain during the seasons of discipline and pruning. Both were knock-down drag-out battles, with God, of course, coming out the winner. Surprisingly enough, I have yet to feel sorry for myself. Every time I felt an impending pity party, my eyes were opened to see someone who was experiencing greater trials.

A forwarded e-mail from a friend titled **For A Reason, A Season, Or A Lifetime,** tells about people who come into our lives to fulfill a special purpose. Years ago, my husband and I were browsing through shops in Carmel, California with my mother-in-law who wanted to buy me a gift. What I chose was something she said would offend people. She gave in and bought it anyway. It is a wall hanging that reads, *All Our Friends Bring Happiness. Some by Coming. Others by Going.* The plaque still hangs on our wall. Just like the e-mail, it is full of truth. There have been people who brought positive changes to my life, while the best thing others could do was leave. Have you known people who call themselves a "best friend"? How many people really were "the best?" How many hurt or deserted you when you needed them the most? When someone is in our life for a reason, we often find they are here to meet a need. The person may have experienced similar trials. This person may need your help and support as much as you need hers. This friendship may last only as long as you need each other.

My friend Hanna came into my life when we were both struggling to live. I give her credit for tying the bow on this package of sanity. Three years into our turmoil here in Bend, I learned of a Southern California couple moving in down the street from us. My neighbor was taking them dinner, and I offered to send a cake.

A few nights later in my home over dinner, I overheard this neighbor telling another about Hanna and how nice we had been to her. She said Hanna was an ovarian cancer survivor and had called that afternoon asking her to stop by and give her a hug. A third victim in her California support group of five had passed away, and she didn't know anyone else in Bend. The neighbor had said she was too busy to acknowledge her request.

I stopped by the next day with the hug she needed. Last Christmas Hanna gave me a doll she said looked like me. "Every time you look and see how beautiful she is," Hanna said, "know that you are that beautiful even if no one ever told you. That little blue-eyed blonde girl inside deserves to be loved and by loving the doll, you will be on your way, my true friend."

Money does play a large part in friendships. When Hanna was feeling well, her calendar was filled with places to go and things to do with other friends who could do the same, which often led to her canceling our plans. I'm convinced God put us in each other's lives for the purpose of helping each other through a rough time. I'm also convinced that God meant it to be short term. Over three years, I learned that some people could fool themselves into believing they are acting Christ like, while they are takers and seldom give back. This realization took its toll on our friendship. Hanna often recited Bible verses to me and made me feel guilty that I wasn't attending church. Two simple incidents showed me it was time to let go.

One day I asked my comfortably retired friend to help me sponsor the student I was mentoring and his two younger siblings. The children were in desperate need of winter clothing and school supplies. "We need to take care of ourselves," she replied. "I have some stickers they can have."

There were several times when Hanna didn't feel well, and I was asked to fix meals. I was glad to do it. Weeks later while recuperating from my own surgery, she did the strangest thing. Hanna asked me out to lunch. After ordering our soup and salads from the counter my wealthy friend returned and asked for my share of $5.50.

I woke the next morning thinking about what I had written about Hanna and my $5.50 luncheon invitation. Why would I write this? The question lingered throughout the morning and into early evening. The more I thought about it, the more ashamed I felt. Driving home from a late piano lesson, I turned off the radio. What's up God? I asked. 1'm sure everyone has experienced something similar more than once, so why is this such a big deal to me? Why am I wasting my time stressing over something so silly at my age? I ran this question past an acquaintance of mine who seems to have all the wrinkles ironed out of his life. "We have very few good friends in life. Many acquaintances. Perhaps your expectations of deep friendship with so many of your human contacts set you up for sadness," he said. I think he may have hit the nail on the head.

There are other people who come into our lives for a season. They can help you grow, teach you to laugh, cry and to love. Sometimes they might be the only ones who can fill a void no one else knows about and when they say good-bye will leave beautiful memories to last forever. Many children went through my Enchanted Playhouse preschool in California, and each child left his or her treasured memory. *There is a time for everything, and a season for every activity under heaven: a time to be born and a time to die, a time to plant and a time to uproot, a time to kill and a time to heal, a time to tear down and a time to build, a time to weep and a time to laugh, a time to mourn and a time to dance --- Ecclesiastes 3:1-4*

Lifetime relationships teach us lessons that will help us when we find ourselves in some of our hardest times. These people strengthen us with their faith and support.

We learn God's greatest lessons in many ways, sometimes amid our suffering. There is no guarantee in God's lesson plan that each step forward won't immediately be followed by two steps back. I didn't want to go to California, but I missed my children. On our way home from the visit, my husband turned into our old neighborhood and drove by the house we had, at one time, planned to own forever. A blanket of bad memories enveloped me. I couldn't breathe, and it felt like my head was on fire. Three weeks later I was still depressed. I missed my children. I had never felt so alone. I wanted a real friend before I went nuts! Somehow, I knew I was searching for a different sort of friendship.

The next day Doris brought her daughter for piano lessons. I had known the family for four weeks. After the lesson I waved good-bye and from my window, I saw the van drive back down the road in reverse, turn the corner, and return to my drive. Doris met me on the porch blushing. "I never do this," she said, "but something wouldn't let me leave before asking you to a Bible study that starts this week in my home." Her invitation was answered with a loud sigh.

Doris had no way of knowing my passion for gardening when she handed me the lesson sheets, **Tending Your Spiritual Garden**. I said very little at that first class. By the fourth gathering, I apologized for unloading my problems on them. That day I saw one of God's most ingenious plans displayed in Doris' living room. Five of the seven women in the group have gone through emotional breakdowns following atrocious financial losses on home construction. I felt so much compassion for these ladies but understood the reasoning behind the blessing God had sent. We really did understand each other's pain.

When we were five weeks into Bible class, I found myself feeling terribly lonely. I missed my children and having our family together. As much as I never wanted to see California again, I called our friend and good realtor, Louie, and asked his advice on selling our home, no matter the loss. Louie thought I was completely out of my mind! I hung up the telephone after talking with him and picked it up again to hear Doris' voice on the other end. "OK," she said, "I know I crossed the line once and now I'm doing it again. I'm inviting you to visit my church when you're ready."

Each Bible study took six weeks to complete. By the end of the third study, I was starting physical therapy for neck pain. I was in the habit of asking God each time I headed into a dark place: "Get me out quickly." The last time I called on Him to help me out of a depression caused by missing my children, I was sure He had yanked me out so fast I got a whiplash. I was learning about the envy I stored in my heart for those who enjoyed the pleasures I thought should have been our reward in retirement. It's all meaningless. God showed me what I didn't need to be happy, but He also tested my forgiveness for those who took it away.

One morning Pastor asked me if I was a Christian. I've never considered myself a Christian, because I've never thought I measured up and because of a problem I've had with going to church. I was never turned off from God, just by the actions of people called Christians. Many times, I would think, "If that's a Christian, I want no part of that club. "Christians aren't perfect," Pastor said. "Just believe in Jesus and God will make it right.

A warm greeting on that first Sunday in the little country church without the bright lights and glitter triggered my curiosity and attending services became a big part of my life. Relationships were growing. I was learning you cannot live until you can love. A fourth Bible study and I had a lot of answers, but I couldn't verbalize anything without becoming a sobbing mess and the box of Kleenex was always shoved my way. Writing my answers in story form and passing them to Doris to read out loud proved to be my best tactic. I still need the box of Kleenex, though.

This morning while sitting in my bedroom, in my purple chair, having coffee with God as I like to think, I caught a glimpse of the second purple chair across the room. This is amazing! When my husband and I were first married, the design for our future bedroom centered around two purple chairs pictured in a Spiegel's catalogue. These plans were soon forgotten. These lovely wing-back chairs have been handed down to us by his mother and they were recently reupholstered in purple! I looked again at these purple chairs. I thought about our little brown house. I knew I was closer to my children than ever before. God is telling me not to chase dreams, that He has much more to give me.

One morning, as I turned to leave Pastor's office, after meeting to discuss church doctrine, he asked if I had been baptized. I had, but it hadn't been my choice of place or time, and it hadn't been for the right reasons. "Sprinkles or the full immersion?" he asked. My answer of sprinkles seemed to amuse him. "Someday we have to get you all the way in," he said as I left the room. Pastor's view on baptism raised a question pertaining to verses in the Book of 1 Peter. ...***God waited patiently in the days of Noah while the ark was being built. In it only a few people, eight in all, were saved through water, and this water symbolizes baptism and now saves you also....1Peter 3:20-21.***

I understood scripture to tell of Noah and his family being in the ark until stepping out on new ground. Nothing was ever mentioned about being immersed fully in the water. I was volunteering at youth group when Pastor announced the upcoming baptism. Baptized with the kids? Am I ready, or are there too many areas that I'm still working on?

I don't like repeating the word "lame," but that feeling is returning. Knowing God wants spiritual fruit, not religious nuts, I wasn't sure if I should share my prayer box. Evidently my stories, Doris reading them aloud, and the box of Kleenex had become a hit in Bible study, so why keep my box a secret? I'm a visual person and I had wanted to see my worries go away. I was sitting in my purple chair when my eyes drifted to a beautiful white box, the size of a child's shoebox, we had received for our thirtieth wedding anniversary. It had sat empty for seven years. I wrote down fifty-seven prayers and dropped them inside.

That evening my daughter e-mailed, "Mom, I need spiritual guidance in my life again." The first on my list of prayers was to know where my daughter's faith was. Two days later my son told me, "Mom, I just received two grants for school." I shared my prayer box with him. I had asked God to let Michael's applications for school loans go through without a hitch. Remembering something I read about "God doesn't want you to ask Him to move hills when He is capable of moving mountains," I had taken the prayer out of the box and added, "Please make it a grant." In a two-week period, I had become a chain Kleenex user and almost dried out my yellow highlighter marking passages in my Bible. My prayers were being answered so fast, I didn't want to fall asleep and miss something. Life sometimes moves too quickly, and I wanted to learn to slow down and discover special moments I might otherwise miss. I had planned to resist answering the phone when I was in quiet time with God, but I was thinking about my prayer box when I asked God to have my son in California call me. Quiet time over, I answered the phone on the first ring. Eric was calling from his classroom which he has never done. He teaches special needs children, and his students sang a song for me. I said, "I love you," when he came back on the phone. Silence, and then I heard him say "I love you Mom, and I miss you so much."

I've gained a reputation for crying. Abby, another friend attending Bible study announced that "When God sent the rainbow as a promise never to send another flood, He forgot about Juanita." So many answered prayers and now I'm learning it's OK to pray for ourselves.

God gave women one law we all fail to obey: Don't worry. Worrying is number one job for all women, and God tells us not to. There was a hush in the room when asked to pray for patience. It seems God may take us through a storm to earn patience.

Faith grows as I live one day at a time, knowing God is with me. *Hope* is waiting for better things to come. *Charity* I give freely without a thank you. *Forgiveness* is a work in progress, and God hasn't given up on me. *Love* I learned to give unconditionally. Having been broken and then put back together, I know who I am, and I love myself for the first time. Joy is delight, beauty, rejoicing, happiness, elate. No matter what word used to describe *Joy*, it brings **Peace**. And if you're not careful, *Joy* can be contagious! *Prayer* is what brings it all together.

It is 6 p.m., and time to take the big plunge with the youth group. Pastor smiles and takes my hand as I walk into the pool. I was told it would be heated yet I'm looking around for ice cubes. Pastor takes my other hand, asks if I'm ready to accept the Lord and down I go. Coming up to a room of smiles, tears and cheering is a beautiful experience, but I didn't feel what I anticipated.

The next morning, I sat in my purple chair and thought about my baptism and the let-down of not feeling what I thought I was supposed to feel. Did I fake my own baptism?? Then God answered my question by opening my eyes to the answers He had sent. God had answered so many of my fifty-seven prayers, almost as soon as they were dropped into my box, because He wanted me to have no doubt as to who He is. I lost it big and loud! It was the morning of the devastating flood! The feeling I anticipated at my baptism blew in like a storm that day.

I was on a natural high for days following my baptism. For the first time in my life I felt like a whole person. I felt I had found my true-identity. Prayers continued to be answered at a rapid pace, and God allowed me to feel His presence on many occasions. I couldn't wait to go to sleep and wake up to what was going to happen the next day. Then it seemed to stop. I sat one morning in my purple chair and asked, "Have I done something wrong?" Had everything in the past couple of weeks been my imagination?" I clung to these questions for several days before confronting my friend Nancy. "That's the peace living in Christ brings," she said," "The things you have been doing for other people are all evidence of your love for God and the peace you have found. It's a sweet-smelling fragrance that goes heavenward! And nothing goes unnoticed by God even if it is sometimes unnoticed by man."

Emily, another friend from church, and I were on our way to visit Maude, an elderly church member who lived in an adult-assistance home, when I explained what I was feeling. "Like your own father, our Heavenly Father carries us through our infancy and then it comes time for us to take our first steps," she said. "The difference is that God never leaves us. Once filled with our Heavenly Father's love and trust, we have joy and peace."

My mind was playing tricks, but my heart knew what Emily had told me was real. Walking down the corridor after returning Maude to her room, I confided in Emily that there are times I'm tempted to take short cuts and ask God for miracles. "Then why don't you?" she said. Was this allowed? It took forever just to ask Him for help and now I'm asking for miracles?

It's a hard night when your brain won't shut down. Taking a mental look at the list inside my prayer box and considering how I would ask God for a miracle; I concluded. These prayers are for the people I love and care the most for in this world, and I want miracles for each of them. If my prayers for these loved ones are answered, there is nothing left to ask God to do for me. My peace is wrapped up in knowing my loved ones are in our Father's care. I laid on my bed and asked Him! "I know

You are able," I said, "and I know it will happen according to Your Will and in Your Timing."

It is 3:45 a.m. and I'm as hyped as I get after an aerobic workout. I think I've just experienced taking a leap in faith. I get out of bed, without waking my husband or my dog, Sissy, and e-mail Emily. God wants spiritual fruit, but if I wake anyone at this time of day, no doubt I will be considered that Religious Nut. I explained to Emily how I have had this feeling five times in my past. The first time was when I heard the priest say, "I pronounce you husband and wife." The second third, and fourth, were when I heard the doctor say, "It's a boy!" "A girl" "A boy!" Number five was the morning after baptism when I accepted knowing God has always protected me. *The Lord does not look at the things man looks at. Man looks at the outward appearances, but the Lord looks at the heart....1Samuel 16:7*

The importance of appearances has been engrained in our minds. But the Lord looks at our hearts. Very simple when you think about it. Why does one go to an expensive dress shop when something of the same quality or better can be found at a thrift store, for much less?

Won't most of you agree that we women love compliments, especially for our appearance? We search for the right makeup and wardrobe to look attractive, yet God holds the secret to becoming a beautiful woman and it takes little work and no money. Once we are able to love, because we know we are loved, it just happens. Friends who hadn't seen me since Christ came into my life would say, "You look different. You look so healthy. What have you been up to?" My son, Michael, told me one day, "Mom you've changed. You're stronger now than you have ever been".

Sharing my faith with my husband isn't an easy task. He is a wonderful man with a big heart and believes in God. But when it comes to a belief of who Christ is, we come from opposite ends of the spectrum. I can feel very alone at times because I want to share with him but not push him past his comfort zone. Although being raised in the Catholic Church and parochial schools has turned him off from church altogether, my husband is the first to acknowledge that my faith and my church have given me a healthier mindset, and he has never failed to support me in every aspect of my life.

When God transforms our hearts, it affects every part of our lives. With the peace that comes from trusting God with our hearts and our lives, so does the understanding of why God allows delays, disappointment and suffering to come our way. If we give God room without time frames to work in our lives then we don't need to see the full canvas of a future before us. As long as our hearts are in the right place and we believe in Christ and know that God loves us, we don't need to understand His power and His majesty. We only must gaze at the stars to believe and if we believe we will learn to hear His whispers in our hearts.

Sitting in the backyard, my eyes drifting from the rock garden filled with white flowers shining in the moonlight to a dark sky filled with twinkling stars, I reflect on my life before Christ. There is no comparison. I had so much then but always felt there had to be something better. Although I didn't see my father as being the strong head of the home, he was possibly the closest person to me outside of David and the kids. He may have thought he was leaving me with nothing but that is far from the truth. He left me his sense of humor. I watched my father live two years in agonizing pain. Each time he recovered from treatments, he and I made jokes and laughed. Sharing laughter was much easier than sharing tears. Laughter and playing "The Glad Game" from the movie Pollyanna helped me through lots of sad times.

God has given us many gifts. Laughter is one of the greatest medicines: We don't need a prescription for and it will never run out. God hands it out freely for anyone who will take it. I've heard it said, "If we ask a creative God, He will help us to open His gift box of laughter." Laughter, sunshine, rainbows and faithful friends, what more can we ask of a loving God to brighten our difficult days?

Do you believe in angels? If so, do they float around on clouds munching on bagels and cream cheese or do you have a different version? I'm afraid to admit I used to vote for the white-robed bagel muncher until I was proven wrong. A good friend had made a sudden move to Michigan and found herself in a desperate situation. She had been convinced by an older friend, whom she had known and trusted for most of her life, to quit her job, give up her apartment and move with her, away from all that was familiar to her. It had been an attempt by the longtime friend to mislead and fraudulently take money from her.

My friend was scared, homeless, and had enough money in her pocket for gas and a meal. She stopped at a pizzeria and, in front of the shop, stood the saddest man she had ever seen, holding a sign reading "This is a sad day in my life." She passed him but then didn't go inside. She walked back and gave the man everything she had except what she needed for a slice of pizza. It was rush hour, and for some unknown reason the manager of the shop gave her a free lunch. She immediately went outside to give the extra money to the sad man with the sign. He was gone.

By the next morning many good things had come to my friend. On the next Sunday, I sat in church listening to the choir sing *We Are Standing On Holy Ground*. I thought about my friend and the kindness she had for the sad man with the sign. I had never considered a pizza shop being sacred ground, but my heart told me this man holding the sign had been my friend's guardian angel. **Do not forget to entertain strangers, for by so doing some people have entertained angels without knowing it. ---Hebrews 13:2**

I believe God places guardian angels in our lives for a variety of reasons: to guide us, to console us, to remind us we have a heart, and to make us laugh. It makes me laugh in wonder to allow my imagination to see people as undercover angels. I know how insane this might sound but think about it. If each of us took to heart and obeyed Matthew 25, what changes would it make to a warped world built on greed and selfishness? **The King will reply, "I tell you the truth, whatever you did for one of the least of these brothers of mine, you did for Me. ---Matthew 25:40**

About six months after we had moved into our new home on the mountain, I turned the local news on one night and listened to an interview with a gentleman in a nearby town. A soft-spoken man like my father, he explained how to enter an essay contest to win his ten-acre ranch. I tried to sleep that night, but the thoughts of the newscast wouldn't let me. I got up from bed and wrote an essay. The next day I counted the coins I had dropped into a bank while in California when money was no object, and I had a total of $160.00. The contest required cashier's check for $150.00 to be sent along with the essay. I heard myself saying over and over: "This is pure craziness on my part. How can I give away this money when I have nothing else?" As soon as I dropped it at the office, I wished the contest would fold and my money would be refunded.

Three days later the phone rang, and an unfamiliar voice said, "So you're from Mason?" He introduced himself as the owner of the ranch. 'My elderly parents live in Junction, Texas" he explained, "twenty minutes from Mason." The man was hoping a contest would speed up the selling of his property and allow him to move to Texas to care for them. I've met people who know of Central Texas, but rarely do I meet people who have heard of Mason. The gentleman talked with me for twenty minutes. I didn't see wings, but he was the angel of comfort I needed. I later received notice that the contest had folded, and a refund was in the mail.

Angels come in all sizes, too! I will share a story about three little angels who came into my life six years ago. Travis was a third grader I mentored in school through the *Study Buddy Program."* Earlier in the week his class field trip had been featured on the front page of the local newspaper. No one had to guess the identity of that happy boy in flying motion. I was walking with the dogs through Drake Park the following Saturday. It was a beautiful afternoon under Central Oregon blue skies and white swans were swimming in the river. What happened next was even more spectacular. A little boy playing in a dirt pile on the baseball field, wearing a bike helmet came running across the field yelling, "I know you! You're my school helper!" Red hair stuck out from under the helmet and sweaty dirt smeared his face-this adorable kid was Travis!

My son, Michael, was also a volunteer and we made an appointment to talk with Travis' teacher when we noticed significant changes in his behavior. Just last week I was asked to come an extra day to mentor, because it was the first time Travis had handed in homework. His teacher asked if we knew anything about Travis, and we didn't. We asked obvious questions and also if she could explain why Travis seemed so determined that I know there is a basket in the office containing book orders. She said he could not afford to order books. This little boy and his two younger siblings are being cared for by their father while their mother is somewhere in town living the life of a drug addict. Travis' father is the main caretaker but can hardly take care of himself because of a problem with alcohol.

We were told that Travis, who is not a violent child, set fire to the boy's bathroom and it escalated into a very big event. Fire fighters and police officers were brought on campus. Travis was taken to see how juvenile hall operates and made to stand up in front of his peers during an assembly and apologize. Travis accepted responsibility for his actions yet had no one to hold onto for comfort and security and most of all to love him unconditionally.

The teacher told us that Travis desperately needed school supplies. Our first stop was Wal-Mart, and we picked up a pencil box and filled it with the school supplies we could afford. It was just a small Band-Aid for his hurts, but it brought a quick smile. We stopped by my friend Julia's house on the way home. Julia immediately wrote out a check for me to use as book-order money for Travis throughout the school year.

I call Travis one of my little angels, but I saw a tangible circle of angels working together for him. My husband and I completed our foster parenting classes and prepared a bedroom with furniture and toys. Two days after being certified I accepted an emergency call to take two little girls. We had asked for five-to-ten-year-old's and received a six-year-old and two-year-old. Immediately following the telephone call a police officer walked in carrying a beautiful blonde haired, blue-eyed baby and leading her sister who was equally striking with flaming red hair and hazel eyes. I had no kid food, so the officer left and returned with McDonald's burgers and fries.

The girls were sitting at the table coloring when my husband came home. A twenty-four-hour emergency foster situation turned into months for us. Although our home was a haven for these children, we soon became part of a lifestyle even our social workers said was mismanaged and catered more to those from whom the children are taken.

Travis and these little girls were the angels of encouragement I needed to write the **Be There For Kids** article for the newspaper in "Blue April." Blue April is when posters are hung around town and speeches made to encourage adults to watch out for the welfare of kids.

I had never done anything like it before and to receive phone calls and letters, even from the state capital, and to know other people shared my feelings, was a good thing. The following is the article that appeared in the newspaper.

Be There For Kids

This morning I received an e-mail from a ten-year-old Bend girl who had been one of my piano students. "If I had a magic wand, I'll tell you what I'd do. I'd pack a dream into a box and send it straight to you. When you get down to it, there's nothing I'd rather do than to send some magic to the one who gives me magic in ordinary life," she said. Hanging on my refrigerator is a handmade thankyou card from a third grader who placed a book order for the first time along with classmates and no longer borrows the teacher's school supplies. I don't ask for a pat on the back but wish for everyone to know kids are the same no matter where they live or what they have.

All children can hurt, most children can be given happiness with little effort, and each child needs to know there is always someone who cares. After moving to Bend, we met many wonderful people, but we also found greed, dishonesty, and denial. I often wonder how a child feels and is able to cope when there is no one to help them understand, "Why me? How do these kids explain the blue ribbons, posters and banners in the month of April and then it's all gone? Children can hurt year-round, so why not let them know we are here for them year-round? Not until I volunteered in one of the many mentor programs in school, was I aware of the number of children who do not have the protection and the everyday necessities that children need. I also saw how easy it is to bring a smile not only to these children, but to my own family. It costs so little and the rewards are grand. Many wait until Christmas to feel good about giving. I ask: "Why wait?"

I saw Maude for the first time two years ago in a classroom on the Central Oregon Community College campus. I sat watching this rather spunky little lady walk across the room to find just the right chair for the long one-day class. The next week there she was, sitting in the senior citizen's building for another class. Looking around the sanctuary my first morning in church, guess who I saw? Maude! Maude is an interesting person to listen to and a very funny person to watch as she drifts off to sleep during some of the pastor's jubilant sermons. The last time this happened, there were two of us prepared to catch her. But then Maude fell in her home and was in serious condition with a head injury in the hospital. Hope for recovery was growing slim.

My husband left on Friday for his annual trip to California for the drag races and our son, who had moved home to help after his father's heart surgery moved out the same day. I carried my dog, Sissy, from my bed to let her outside at 1:30 a.m. for a potty break. I sat her on the ground and she collapsed. I made a frantic and futile call to animal emergency at 7:30 a.m. Saturday morning. twenty-four-hour emergency, and they were closing at 8:00 a.m.? I set out looking for help, but every place was closed.

I kept telling God I wasn't ready to lose both Sissy and Maude. I asked Him to please wait. As massive hysteria sat in, I drove past a veterinarian's office and stopped when I saw a medical assistant dumping trash outside the building. The vet's office was opening and I went in. Placing Sissy on the ground outside my car, she collapsed. Minutes before being called to see the vet, I placed her on the floor, and she ran for the door. Do you know how it feels to have a child with a high fever and have it gone away before the doctor has time to examine him or her?

The doctor sat on the floor with Sissy and found nothing wrong with her. She put Sissy on top of the table and again found no injury. I remembered something. Three years ago, our boys left home at Christmas. Sissy watched one go to the airport, and another to the bus depot carrying luggage. Later I had to rush Sissy to the vet with a terrible limp. The assistant then put Sissy on the floor. She looked at me and said, "Oh my, Sissy's holding up the wrong foot." Sure enough, she was!

"I can take X-rays and run blood tests," the understanding veterinarian said, "but what I think is happening here is a case of detachment anxiety." First thing Sissy did when we came home was run for the cookie jar. The next morning came, and who walked in during Pastor's Mother's Day service? Maude! God had given me extra days with these two angels of humor.

It was Tuesday morning and I had a break between piano lessons and the start of a busy afternoon schedule. I sat down in my purple chair, put my feet up, and started to read Secrets of the Vine, by Bruce Wilkinson. My mind was wandering back to yesterday's topic in Bible study. Joy, a powerful three letter word. When I think of joy, I think of peace, and wonder if I will ever find it.

I continued reading until I got to page thirty. It read: "Picture yourself walking through the day (You may even feel like sprinting or running to make it more realistic)! Look over your list of tasks, routines and people who depend on you. Every activity represents a good work for you to walk in - a work that is yours to do, and yours to give to the Lord. You just have to be ready to see it and be ready to do it with your whole heart."

I put the book down for a brief moment and then tried to continue. No matter how hard I tried to read past this paragraph I couldn't, and I knew why. For weeks I've been making excuses not to visit Charlie because I'm scared. Charlie is an older gentleman who lives on our street, and one of the first people I met in our new neighborhood. He always introduces me as "the little lady who was crying when I met her." It was the morning after our nightmare move, and I couldn't do anything but cry! Charlie patted my hand and told me, "You are the blessing this neighborhood has been waiting for." He is such a caring man and so knowledgeable about almost everything. I was visiting him at least every other day before my schedule got so busy. Charlie is in his fourth year of suffering from Lou Gehrig's Disease. Watching my father and my mother-in-law suffer, it was becoming more difficult for me to see Charlie in pain and not doubt God's plans. I decided to put the book down and put on my shoes. I grabbed two chocolate Easter eggs from my piano bag and walked out the door and down the street to Charlie's house.

Joy was seeing Charlie's face and hearing laughter when I handed him and his wife Fran their foil- wrapped chocolate eggs. Charlie asked how I was doing and I said, "After almost a lifetime of searching, I've found a church where I connect with it and the people." He was happy for me. Charlie asked about the kids, and I shared with him my prayer box and the number of prayers answered in just a week. He smiled and said, "You know you are always in MY prayers." This beautiful man, my angel of love, who called me the blessing the neighborhood had been waiting for and now so close to death, is praying for me! I stayed for about an hour. I'm not sure, but I don't think my feet were touching the ground as I walked home.

I've heard it said that true friends are those who walk in when other's walk out. I would think angels are those who walk in and stay with you no matter what. On a trip to the mountains for a day of exploring, I turned to my friend Cricket and asked the same question I had asked God that morning. "If we don't have the Holy Spirit in us to guide us before accepting Christ as our Savior, then how did I make it this far? Did I have my own Guardian Angel with me all my life?" Cricket just smiled.

"The Lord is My Shepard"....
Psalms 23:1

I've always been a "I don't need any help. I can do this myself" kind of person. Reading through *Traveling Light For Mothers* by Max Lucado, I find it hard comparing myself to a sheep. Mr. Lucado defines sheep as dumb, dirty, and totally dependent on the shepherd. He describes the shepherd as loving and always protecting his flock. It didn't take long to understand God is my Shepherd and He is always in control. Joy is knowing I am unconditionally loved and protected in His flock.

When my husband was in high school, he raised sheep in the Future Farmers of America. My husband also describes them as the dumbest animals he ever met. But dirty? Not David's sheep. One summer he and a family friend decided to bathe the sheep in Woolite before showing them in the county fair. David's name was called, the sheep escaped, and the audience watched in awe at the young man chasing the softest, whitest sheep ever seen in that arena.

"I Shall Not Be in Want" ....
Psalms 23:1

"If I knew then, what I know now, when I was younger, when I was stronger," sang Rod Stewart, in a new release. These words are part of a rock-and-roll song that pumps me up, and I sing along every time I hear it on the radio. My life has been wasted on cravings to satisfy fulfillments. I had everything, but nothing made me feel completely happy. Nothing made me feel like that one complete person I wanted to be.

One morning as I walked out to Tumalo Road, I told God everything I wanted for my husband and my children. I even put the prayers in order of what they needed and what I wanted for them. On the walk back I said, "OK God, now it's my turn." The strangest thing happened; I couldn't think of anything I wanted for myself. What I wanted more than anything was to have my prayers answered for my family. God knows what we need when we don't.... ***"content in every circumstance"*** is all He asks of us.

God's pruning and weeding in my life the past two years has paid off. There are those who may never learn that you can't take your riches with you. When it's your turn to leave this world, you take only what you came in with, and I don't know of anyone born wearing as much as a diaper. Joy is my wealth, and I have a sneaking suspicion after sharing it here on earth, God will let me bring some of it home with me.

"He Makes Me Lie Down in Green Pastures"
Psalms 23:2

"It will never get done if I don't do it! It won't be done correctly if I don't do it. My schedule is tight, but of course I can do it!" My life is filled with obligations and commitments. Raking in praises for being

Super Mom and Super Wife and Super Friend, I sometimes feel a tiny part of me resenting my busy life. I feel tired and sometimes taken advantage of. Sometimes I wish I had the courage to ask someone else to do it! By slowing down and focusing on God, I am discovering that life goes on with or without me. Learning to slow down and say "no" is another one of God's precious gifts that allows a new perspective on living. I admit, I haven't mastered this gift, but I keep on trying.

"He Leads Me by the Still Waters"
Psalms 23:2

Suffering from acute anxiety attacks is proof that worrying solves nothing. An invitation to a Bible study introduced me to a pastor and a church family holding the answer key to my questions. After the death of her mother, a friend was rummaging through her mother's dishes and found an antique box holding an old baby spoon and a yellowed newspaper clipping. The clipping read: *"Today is mine. It is unique. Nobody in the world has one exactly like it. It holds the sum of all my past experiences and all my future potential. I can fill it with joyous memories or ruin it with fruitless worry. If painful recollections of the past come into mind, or frightening thoughts of the future, I can put them away. They cannot spoil today for me. It is mine."* The Shepherd will carry us on a restful path if we only follow.

"He Restores My Soul"
Psalms 23:3

Repeatedly He does restore my soul. I wish that every time God speaks to me, a bell would ring. Don't you know that at the rate He's been answering my prayers, our little church would be packed on Sundays to hear the symphony? Once in my life, fear, anxiety, disappointment, and anger almost destroyed me. Once I gave up on ideas and solutions and had no energy to continue living. It was a time of hopelessness when the word hope was something nasty to flush down the toilet. I denied God's existence. My Gentle Shepherd led me off these broken paths onto the one He leads me on today. Every time I want to give up, He provides just enough hope to keep me on His chosen path. God knows when I'm ready to pick up the pace and take bigger steps to follow Him. Hope is never too small a blessing to ask of God.

"Oh, that you would bless me today indeed"
Chronicles 4:10

Yesterday I awoke with an attitude. I had received cards from three families, all filled with stories of recent travels and perfect children and how God has blessed them throughout the year. Funny, I remember reading that same line on previous cards. For a shameful hour I was envious of these people whom I love. "Why doesn't God bless me and my family in these ways?" A phone call from a piano parent thanking me for how well her children did at a recent recital and a note from a friend saying she misses my smile, began erasing these negative feelings. The morning began with a cup of coffee and a bad attitude, but I soon remembered God blesses each of us every day, indeed He blesses us a lot.

"And enlarge my territory"
1 Chronicles 4:10

Whatever is on my mind when I fall asleep at night is usually still there when I open my eyes in the morning. I tossed and turned in bed last night trying to make sense of the strong will I have for what I'm doing. I'm invited to a going-away dinner at a local restaurant tonight with people from my mountain- top neighborhood. A night with wealthy people sharing stories of travel and adventures I have nothing to add to. I ask God for an attitude adjustment before leaving home. My friend is moving to the Philippines, and it will possibly be the last time I see her. I have a gift but hesitate to give it to her.

While I'm struggling through stories of perfect lives, a lady I had never met mentioned something about prayer. I reached down into my bag and brought out Secrets of the Vine and handed it to my friend. The lady who mentioned prayer said with a smile, I didn't know you were a Christian." When I said "Yes, I am and I was recently baptized with a bunch of little kids, she said "Me too!"

I would discover later when invited to join her in a morning hike, that husband #1 had been a wealthy businessman. Husband #2, the President and CEO of one of the oldest and elite credit card companies in the world. I can't remember much about husband # 3, but she was currently in a miserable marriage to husband #4 and needed someone to talk to before losing her mind. Just goes to show us money seldom buys the sort of happiness we long for.

Another lady who had been very quiet spoke up and shared how she had asked me to put a prayer for her terminally ill husband in my box. Conversation shifted from them to scriptures in the Bible relating to events happening in each of our lives. One of my all-time favorite hymns is In Moments Like These. This gathering became one of these moments *"That Your hand would be with me and would keep me from evil, so I can cause no pain"*...

1 Chronicles 4:10

I believe it's OK to ask God to keep all the bad stuff from us before it tempts us in the first place. There is a purpose in everything we do, including writing a story. I'm beginning to wonder if knowing the purpose is as important as doing the job.

It was 9:25 a.m. Sunday morning July 6, 2003. Seven years from the day I first moved to Bend. I'm late for church but as I got into my car, I felt the need to have Kleenex with me, and I ran back for some. I never carry Kleenex. As I stepped out of my car an eerie feeling encircled my body. Walking into the fellowship hall just as the congregation was entering the chapel, the uncanny feeling remained with me. Pastor began his sermon, and something told me: "This man is resigning today." He announced he had gotten up that morning and made the decision to resign. It came as a total shock, and I wasn't the only one reaching for Kleenex.

An evening meeting had been scheduled for members to meet with the pastor. A husband and wife were asked to leave the church and accused of causing a division and having an agenda to take over the church. Half the church followed them.

Two weeks after his resignation, my crying came to an end when I experienced something I can't explain. I went out walking one evening, which is not unusual. I was alone, and it was getting dark, but I was quite comfortable. As I walked, I thought over my Bible study homework assignment when the idea of using a portion of my story as a testimony popped in my head. Brilliant! I thought of what I could say in my testimony to show both my sorrow for the pastor leaving and my anger for the people who had left our church. I passed the last house before venturing farther down the road. That same eerie feeling I had in church the morning of the pastor's resignation was now smothering me. I had chills and my breathing was shallow. I continued to walk convinced this odd feeling would pass.

The face of the lady who was asked to leave our church suddenly appeared in front of me. Her eyes were black and cold. During the last Bible study this woman had attended something spooky had happened. She turned to me and said, "I know all about you." "Really?" I jokingly replied, "And I know all about you." "No, you don't," she said. "How do you know I am who I say I am, how do you know my name is what I say it is?" Those piercing black eyes went through me like a spear and oddly, I felt scared driving home alone. I tried to continue my walk, but my feet didn't want to go any farther. I turned and ran crying all the way home. Once inside I cried until there were no tears left.

I've never been part of a church division, and I never want to be involved in one again. Two weeks after my experience on the walk, I sat in the backyard with my Bible and a mind full of questions. Why had the evening meeting been scheduled a week before his resignation, when Pastor said he woke up and made the decision that morning? I had many questions and none of the answers made sense. Something wasn't right.

Two months after the division, I was driving home when I begged God to give me some insight into the church split. I had begun to feel like a puppet whose strings were being pulled by those who remained at the church. It was a direction in which I wasn't sure I wanted to go. Two hours later I turned on my computer and a name I have done business within the past appeared on the screen. The address I recognized immediately as being Pastor's previous business address. I phoned the person whose name appeared on my computer with questions concerning our Pastor and was given the missing facts.

God has repeatedly told us in the Bible that no one is perfect. Like so many of us, Pastor made some stupid choices in his personal life which drastically affected his position in the church. Instead of calling for an open question and answer time with all the accused and the congregation, Pastor allowed church leaders to place total blame on someone else and gave room to gossip erupting like a volcano. I don't know what that evening walk and the vision of the woman was all about, but I'm sure it had to do with searching for the truth.

Two years went by with me feeling like the "Push Me-Pull You" character from the original Doctor Doolittle movie. I wanted to hold on to my little country church but felt I couldn't hold my tongue much longer. God is pleased to see our faith as we help people. Sometimes our service comes as a smile or a listening ear. I was in the middle of an agonizing situation since the division and couldn't hear God instructing me. I hadn't spoken out with the information I have and was aware that I could destroy the hearts of some and heal the hearts of others and I have loved ones on both sides. Would this be a service to these people or would it be more than what God was calling me to do? Or was He even calling me to do anything at all?

An old-timer in the church said to me one morning after Sunday services, "The devil must have picked the ex-Pastor up by his feet and given him a good shaking." She welcomed the Pastor back with open arms when he walked in on Christmas morning to be part of the congregation. The old-timer refuses to forgive the other members who asked to return, who were told they would have to stand before the congregation and repent of their sin. The ex-Pastor was never asked to do this.

We often wonder why God's timing is so slow. "He may seem slow to us, but He's never late. If the matter was handled correctly the church will grow," said a Pastor from another church. "If not, the church will never heal. "Two years passed since the division and twenty members fill the sanctuary on Sunday mornings while neighboring churches are full.

I see no sign of our church healing. Looking around the sanctuary I see the new Pastor and the faces of twenty members. My heart has been slowly hardening to words and actions of shunning which I will not accept as God's way. You can be the most zealous Christian who wants to please God and do the right thing, but your zeal needs to be channeled in the right direction. Your thoughts and behavior may need to be adjusted to walk wisely in God's ways, not mankind's.

I have sat at my computer for what seems like days, writing, deleting, and praying for God to take this burden from me and do it Himself. I finally went to work in my rock garden. I should have thought of it sooner. God often speaks to me in my garden. Of course, it's where I often disclose some of my most inner thoughts and questions. 'Today the only thing on my heart is how do I do this? How do I write about a church I love but have lost respect for? How do I do this without saying I am right and they are wrong? "What am I looking for in a church?" I ask.

I want a church that will light the flame in me I once felt before it burns out entirely. I want a pastor who will teach from a biblical view, and not fill sermons and Bible studies with personal thoughts and feelings and expect the congregation to follow without being questioned. I want a church that believes God gave each of us a heart and a brain and expects us to use them to show others how glorious He is and maybe how glorious we can be in His image.

I want a church that believes if Jesus were walking amongst us today, He would not shun people. Knowing people from as many walks of life as I do, I know there are detestable and disgusting people in every lifestyle. I want a church that believes in God's Word and believes we are not to just love certain types of people. How do we know God is not testing our love for all sorts of people who are not on the list of desirables? On almost every page of the Bible God tells us to love one another. I want a church where the congregation takes time to know a person and to love him. If it is God's will, He will work through the church to bring that person closer to Him. There is so much we cannot fathom about God's plans and what a relief to know He is not expecting it.

God doesn't want us to be religious robots. I went to church and prayed for strength to make wise choices. I left empty and lackluster. I felt like the victim on a ship that was sinking fast. I left that little country church, where I had come to know Christ, for good that morning. I was now an outsider from "the club" and tempted to title this chapter *Faith in Relationship Where Satan Gets His Licks In!*

A month passed before I visited another church. To say I felt overwhelmed doesn't do this church justice. My eyes rolled, and my ears buzzed when coming from a quaint country atmosphere. The church is held in a nearby school gym. It began as a Bible study in the home of the pastor who had branched off from another church. At six months the gym was half full. At one year the gym is overflowing. This morning's sermon is in Chapter Three of Revelation and to my surprise, I sit wondering how it is possible to feel so happy, hearing something that gave me a migraine the first time I studied it?

This pastor has a warmth about him you feel from a distance and his soothing voice makes you want to soak in everything he says. He may rehearse hours each week, but you would never know because of the love for God that pours out. I smile as I hear the pastor say, "Presentation of God's Word is important." The pastor began this morning with God's instructions on bringing people to Him. "Take time and get to know the person, "he said. "Love the person, and if it is God's plan, we will bring that person closer to Him." No shunning. Just love them!

Something very strange is happening to me. I feel like I've been through a great earthquake and now I have to deal with the aftershocks. Despite visiting the new church, weeks are going by, and I don't even want to read my Bible. My mind seems to be out of focus, and I feel detached from God. I really can't seem to pray at all. I'm beginning to understand what it means to ask God to provide our daily bread, all things necessary for life. When I felt this way before, I was deeply depressed. I'm okay with my choice to leave the country church, where I first came to personally know Christ. I am delighted with the freedom I feel at not being in the middle. I'm hurting though, because I've left the only real family I've known outside of David and the kids, but I don't want to go back. God tells us He will never give us more than what we can handle and knowing He is on my side I know I can move forward and grow strong.

If God never gives me another challenge, I will stay busy the rest of my life trying to understand His command to be content. Contentment in the dictionary is defined as being satisfied or having a mind at ease.

Unfortunately, it seems I seldom have either. I was born with a strong resolve, and I don't know if I should call it a blessing or a curse. I've always wanted to jump in the middle and solve a problem NOW! Don't beat around the bush. Call everyone together in a locked room and get to the bottom of things immediately. Amazing how many people I've met who don't think the way I do.

If I were to define the word "gossip," it would mean two-sided stories, destroyed relationships and discontentment. God wrote my life story before I was born and as difficult as that was to accept, I did understand that mistakes and regrets are meant to serve a purpose. I even understand and accept that the purpose is to be able to help others through the same trials. On my kitchen wall hangs a plaque I purposely hung in a spot I must look at every day. It's a favorite verse of mine and may be what keeps me from giving up on finding contentment. The plaque reads: *"For I know the plans I have for you," declares the Lord, "Plans to prosper you and not to harm you, plans to give you hope and a future." ---Jeremiah 29:11*

The pastor at my new church says most Christians have questions concerning our Heavenly Father's plans. "Just take a look at the world and see the suffering and pain inflicted on innocent people, especially the children. But we need to be content having these questions go unanswered." One morning I sat in my purple chair, and I began praying. I was so bogged down in unanswered questions I kneeled beside my bed, and I argued with God. It was the first time I had ever kneeled to pray, and I felt my Father kneeling there with me. "God I may be in deep trouble talking this way," I said, "but I need to be honest with You." I argued, and I cried. I poured out my complaints and my disappointments, and what I wanted in my life to make it perfect.

I went to sit in the backyard. It was a perfect setting in which to regroup after debating with someone I never in my wildest imagination would have said these things to. Birds chirped at the feeder, flowers of all colors waltzed in a light breeze, and those beautiful Central Oregon skies were as blue as ever. Reflecting on my prayer, I saw God to be a good friend who had knelt beside me and listened to my ranting and raving. I saw I had asked for nothing new, absolutely nothing had been added to this prayer. But this time everything I've asked for was bundled together in one package. All my wishes were for my loved ones. Things I wanted for them and basics they need, nothing extravagant. Except, I must admit because I wasn't holding anything back, I did ask God to send a grandchild while my feet are still planted on this side of the grass!

My Webster's defines peace as being in a tranquil state. A Bible dictionary defines peace as a state of security. The Bible tells us God is behind the scenes of human suffering; that God may not answer our questions about life's suffering; that He will never give us more than we can handle. There will come a time and I believe not too far away, when we look into the beautiful face of Jesus, a brilliant emerald rainbow crowning His head, and we will ask our questions and get our answers. I've carried a bookmark with me like a child carries a security blanket. It shows Sally Forth running as if her world has been flip- flopped and underneath, she says, *I'm Learning to Take Life One Disaster at a Time!* Until Christ's glorious return, the only thing I can do is deal with the disasters and keep a list of the questions.

Days go by when *I'm The Little Engine Who Could.* I have an attitude of "I think I can" or "I know I can," and then comes the day when I ask myself, "Can I?" These are the days I remind myself of something I read: "The Lord is like the ocean. You can see the beginning but not the end." I have to keep driving forward, not putting myself in reverse or allowing myself to stay neutral. Following a fourth cancer scare I wondered if I would be the one to write the ending to this chapter or if it would be one of my children. They may have things to add, but God is the one who will write the final page.

We've had great travels to Europe, Alaska, Hawaii and the Caribbean Islands planned and canceled due to family emergencies. Funny, I've always felt like I was going to explode from anticipation experiencing life by traveling and venturing into new territories. Luckily, no explosion has emerged from unfulfilled dreams. Last summer my friend, Marilyn, arranged for us to spend a week at Whistler Village in Canada for my birthday this year. I woke at 3:30 a.m. five months ago and said I can't go. I think this was God sharing His sense of humor again. He had given me a greater gift than any vacation I could have dreamed of: Being with my daughter when she gives birth to my grandchild, due on my birthday, and nine months after praying on my knees!

My husband and I walked out to Tumalo Road this evening. He teased me about turning sixty in a few months. Aging has never bothered me. Tonight, I wondered how many years I have left. "When I leave this planet" I commented, "I will have traveled nowhere, and I will be able to write my adventures on a Post-it. I don't think so!" replied David. "Unlike most people, I think every day is an adventure for you."

PART 2

Season of Pruning

I Found What I Was Looking For

He replied, "Because you have so little faith, I tell you the truth, if you have faith as small as a mustard seed, you
can say to this mountain, 'Move from here to there,' and it shall move. Nothing will be impossible for you.
----Matthew 17:20

    Do you ever wish you could turn back the hands of time? I have when thoughts of "What if?", "I should have," or "If only" slip into my thinking. Satan uses our regrets as strong tools to take our focus off Jesus. Once we believe the truth about Jesus, that He died on the cross for our regrets, Satan must release his foothold on our lives. "He paid a debt He did not owe. We owed a debt we could not pay." These words that we sing in church on Sunday morning say it all.

    It has been eight years since I invited Christ into my heart. I'm still a "baby Christian." All my steps seem to be infant sized as my faith grows. I understand "God's Season of Discipline." Many times, during this process, though, I've not trusted God to come through for me. Surprisingly enough, He was OK with it. Instead of losing patience He teaches me to listen for His gentle whispers. My God has a plan and a purpose for me. With each sunrise He gives me a new day of adventure. He gives me gifts and talents. When I cannot grasp what these gifts and talents are, knowing how to listen is a gift in itself. Going through "God's Season of Pruning," the reality of Him always at my side is comforting. I'm thankful for a childlike faith.

I found one of God's blessings to be writing short stories. Putting on a bright face when I felt miserable wasn't easy, but the writing seemed to lighten my load. I've never taken writing seriously but sitting at the computer punching out words possibly saved my life. While friends and neighbors boasted of adventures past and present and worldly pleasures to come, I typed.

The Rag

Twenty years ago, I walked into our bathroom and found the old piece of torn T-shirt my husband used to polish his uniform shoes, on the countertop. Instead of putting it in the laundry, I dropped it into his bathroom drawer. That night I found it in the fitted sheet on my side the bed. Knowing it was going to be a sunny morning when David left for work, I sneaked outside in my nightgown at 5:30 a.m. while he was showering and placed the rag on the sun visor of his car. As he drove away, I watched from a kitchen window as he pulled down the visor, and the rag fell into his lap. The game did not end there.

I have found the rag in some surprising places, but my husband does not outwit me. One Valentine's Day, I enlisted the help of a downtown storeowner on David's delivery route. My husband walked into the shop, and she asked him to wait, she had something for him. Eleanor handed him a beautiful Valentine gift bag with a wrapped gift inside. Customers stood by watching as he carefully opened his special Valentine gift, while saying, "Thank you Eleanor, you shouldn't have." He slowly pulled out the rag!

My husband was called over the intercom to come to the front desk during a bowling tournament. With a crowd watching, he was handed a large envelope containing what he thought was a bowling award. In the quiet of the crowded room, David pulled out the rag!

Christmas 1999, I spotted a beautifully wrapped present under the tree with my name on the tag. I tore at the wrapping paper. I could feel the excitement rising. Here it is. That precious rag making us laugh. The following Christmas Eve we went to Schezuan, a favorite restaurant downtown Bend, for dinner. A family member came out and presented us with tiny glimmering Christmas bags and said something in Chinese. We looked inside and found gifts wrapped in colorful Asian paper. I opened mine to find a brightly colored tree ornament. My husband opened his to find...the rag!

God doesn't always answer in the way we want, but He does answer. We need to keep our eyes and hearts open, so we are ready to be taught by God. Remaining on those mountain tops, times in my life when I had no unbearable stress and a lifetime of dreams coming true, would have been my first choice. Knowing it was not part of God's plan is where I am. Understanding why I am far better off for not being on a comforting mountain top is taking longer. Understanding why my life seems like a long, drawn-out soap opera with me as drama queen, is taking a long time, too.

I've seen my vocabulary change since beginning this story. I've seen it grow from puny to-not-so -puny in a reasonably small measure of time. A Bend pastor recommends keeping an old-fashioned dictionary next to our Bible. The Bible contains beautiful words, but without the meanings, they are mere words. Take for instance the word "omnipotence," God's all-powerful nature to do anything. The word "omnipresence" means God's ability to know and see everything and to be everywhere at once.

Some would say my family is lucky, but I say it was God's plan. Car seats hadn't been invented when our oldest son, Eric, was a toddler. He stood behind my right shoulder as I pulled up to a railroad crossing. After looking both ways, I crossed over. As the back of my car pulled off the tracks, I heard a loud whistle blast, and, in my rear-view mirror, I saw flashing red lights as the rapidly moving train raced by.

My husband was out riding his bike when I received the phone call from the hospital. A physician's wife, in a hurry to leave on vacation, had run a stop sign, throwing David in the air and onto the hood of her car. Panicking, she threw the car in reverse, dragging our baby who was strapped in the infant carrier. Both my husband and Michael received Band-Aids on their scrapes.

On Sunday evening, our pastor walks in bringing our daughter, Annette, home from a church camping trip. We had been unable to attend and entrusted her to the care of church leaders. "I am so sorry," the pastor announced. Adults with no common sense had put our twelve-year-old daughter, who had never been white- water rafting, into a raft with her ten-year-old friend who was as clueless as herself and sent them on their way down the river. Our daughter was thrown from the raft, carried under a bridge and the strap of her life jacket caught on a jagged rock. Looking up from beneath the water and seeing panic on faces looking down, she knew she was drowning. A high school boy risked his life to jump in and save her. If her jacket had come loose on its own, she would have been pulled under the bridge where no one could have reached her.

I flew with Eric to Ohio to chaperone a color guard competition. I sat outside the hotel waiting for the kids to pack up and get on the bus for the ride to the airport. Bewildered faces let me know something shocking had taken place. While standing on the second-story balcony, our son had taken a step backward to let someone pass. He had fallen and landed on his back on the first-floor stairway. God must have placed the other mother there to cushion my son's body. Amazingly, he was in perfect condition and the blessed cushion had only a few bruises to brag about. It is a miracle. I never know if I should laugh or cry when I tell the story.

I lived with colon cancer. I got my affairs in order and was planning my funeral. I was scared. I was numb. How would David and the children hold up through this ordeal of seeing me sick and then leaving them? Seven months later I was told it was a mistake. You might think God would give it a rest. A few months later, watching the eyes of the X-ray technician was not comforting. Trying not to sound alarmed, she excused herself to get the radiologist who after viewing the screen, insisted I see a specialist that day. The doctor would not know if it was ovarian cancer until she operated. I woke up to smiles on the surgeon's face and her whisper, "No cancer girl, but you must have a high tolerance for pain." David kissed my cheek and said, "Can't you ever do something simple?" I know God's hand was on me in the operating room, wearing a smile and telling me: "Maybe now you believe I have great plans for you."

Love You Forever, by Robert Munsch. What a book. I have dozens of stories to tell about this little book ostensibly written for children. I first heard of it from one of my admirable preschool moms who had received it as a Christmas gift. On the way home, in the car on Christmas Day, her five-year-old twin boys asked her to read it to them. A few pages into the story, Lori began sobbing and her husband pulled off the freeway, thinking she was sick. It was just the book making her cry. John, her husband, promised the boys he would read it when they got home. That was the last I heard of the book until two years later at their daughter Gabby's third birthday party. We were standing around discussing books, and I asked John what he thought of *Love You Forever,* and he said, "I don't know. I've never been able to finish it."

One day while browsing through Walden Book Store in Eastridge Mall, I spotted Love You Forever and began to read it, After the first few pages, I put the book down and left the crowded store crying, I went back to buy the book and tried to read it to the preschoolers. I started to weep every time. Finally, I asked Jessica, my second grader, to read the book aloud to the younger children. I waited outside the classroom door. During a final attempt to have my mother's family together for a traditional Thanksgiving holiday, I told them about the book. No surprise to me, eyes rolled, and I was laughed at. I handed the book to my younger sister and said, "Read it." I disappeared into the house. When I came out, I could hear another sister sobbing in the yard. My younger sister was crying while continuing to read out loud.

The Walking Shoes

It is the night of February 26, 2000. The night of Eric's thirty-third birthday. I feel thirty-nine until I remember the ages of my children. A surprise for me tonight, on his birthday, is the special dance Eric choreographed for the evening's program at the university. It was dedicated to me!

His dance partner, Lisa, stepped out to read a part of *Love You Forever*. College students came on stage dressed in bibbed overalls and pigtails, carrying large playground rubber balls. Lisa came out again and continued to read, followed by another playful dance. I was doing very well at controlling my emotions up to that point. My son, Eric, walked out on stage with Lisa and began to read. As the dance followed, my deep breaths became increasingly shallow. When Eric and Lisa returned to read the last part of the story, my daughter stroked my right arm and said, "It's OK Mom."

My husband, sitting on the other side of me, rubbed my shoulder, and my son, Michael, immediately looked over at me with concern. When the lights came up, I was out of there. When I see my son, I turn away. I feel him holding me, my face buried in his sweater crying. He says, "Its OK Mom." In the midst of struggles this world throws at us, God reminds us of the blessings. Eric's recovery from near death in the trauma unit a few months earlier, is one such blessing. "Happy Birthday son. We Love You Forever." ***A time to weep and a time to laugh, a time to mourn and a time to dance ---Ecclesiastes 3:4***

I used to throw out an abundance of one-liner prayers: "God help me to pass this test; God help me to get that; God don't let me have cancer." Sound familiar? I'm learning to take my time when talking to God and have found a Father who loves me and cares about me. Every morning I ask God to stay close to me. To guide me in the direction He wants me to go and, if I slip and fall, to pick me up. I sometimes find myself going to God and apologizing for boring prayers. On the other hand, I know it doesn't matter what we say, because He knows our hearts. God reassures me when my thoughts are scrambled, and He still listens when my words make no sense.

Prayers can bring unimaginable results, especially when they come quickly. "Don't be filled with happiness when your enemy falls." Interesting words spoken in the Bible. Sometimes I wonder if I'm witnessing answers to bad situations or if I am being misguided. A true Christian would never pray for these answers. Our bad California neighbor's son was shot to death. Our bad realtor has cancer. The person in charge of the architectural review board has brain cancer. Another person involved in our construction scam had a massive heart attack. Our crooked contractor built a house for people who could afford to take him to court and did.

Two neighboring families, who had become friends, dropped us like hot potatoes as soon as they knew our financial situation. One of these friends took in a woman and her young son only to discover she had befriended her husband's mistress. A vicious divorce followed. The closeness between the other family, a young doctor and his wife, changed two years later as soon as their social status grew, and their new home was built on the more expensive side of the mountain. The new home was lost after the husband was dismissed from his medical position.

Another woman told me she makes it a habit not to listen to other's problems. It brings her down. Living a life of the very rich, her husband is dying of cancer and their fortune is slipping away. How did I pray for people who hurt me and have no remorse? My first reaction was not a good one. Here I am with Satan on one shoulder whispering "They deserve it" but perched on the other shoulder sits an angel whose gentle voice says, "God wants you to be in His image and what you're feeling is not what God wants." I read somewhere, "If you are feeling heat from the fire, remember that God has His eyes on you and will keep watching you until He sees His image in you". My heart made the right choice and God's wisdom gave me the words to pray.

Driving home from the grocery store one day, my mind was rushing in anticipation of our daughter coming the next day to visit. Coming to a stop, waiting for the signal light to change, I remembered I didn't pray before leaving home, so I did right then. God listens to our hearts when we are knee-deep in errands, busy traffic, or pity parties.

I felt frustrated from not being financially prepared to make fun plans for my daughter's visit. "I have my suitcase packed and I'm ready to go anytime God wants to come and get me," I told my friend Cricket, since there will be no frustration in heaven. "Silly, we won't need a suitcase," she said with a laugh. Cricket is right. The Bible tells us when Jesus returns and takes us with Him, it will be in a twinkle of an eye and everything is left behind.

Roaring thunder and bolts of lightning turn night skies bright. As the storm grows more intense, I wonder how Alfred Hitchcock would begin the next page in my story. I feel like a mindless body passing through space. The only color I saw looking in the mirror was gray. I didn't want this life anymore.

Resting In His Arms

The Sovereign Lord has given me His Words of wisdom, so that I know what to say to all these weary ones.
Morning by morning He wakens me and opens my understanding to His will.
---Isaiah 50:4

Charlie, the gentleman I spoke of earlier in the story, has passed on to a much better place. I remember being devastated learning he was in his second year of Lou Gehrig's Disease. I would watch another three years pass as this disease destroyed my friend's body, but he never let it be a stumbling block in his Christian journey.

One day I had walked down to visit and found Charlie sitting on his back deck watching his wife, Fran, gardening and listening to the boisterous chirping of birds at the feeder. "How's your writing coming along?" Charlie asked with a big smile on his face. He was one of the few with whom I had shared my writing. I was embarrassed to share with Charlie what an editor once told me to do with my story. "People want to read about famous people" the editor had said quite sarcastically. Charlie, still smiling with that never-ending twinkle in his eyes, reached for my hand and said "Go for it kid! Don't let anyone stop you. God will be with you and who is more famous than God?"

It has been six months since I lost my precious dog Sissy. God knows the languages of love and mine was having a spunky little dachshund at my side for sixteen years. I held Sissy as the veterinarian gave the injection and my heart sank to the floor as she took her last breath. Handing her over to the assistant was unbearable. Being a loving God, He soon gave me another love to ease my broken heart. Our daughter was expecting our first grandchild on mine and her great-grandfather's birthdays.

Last Spring while sitting with a neighbor in my rock garden, I said "Things are going well for us. I give God credit, but I can't help but wonder what surprises He has in store". I've decided to trust God with whatever plans He has for me. I'll try hard not to get frustrated. I have no control over my life anyway. So why worry? Why be angry? Why not put all the negative energy into positive thinking? I often wonder if persevering through a stream of hardships means whiter robes and brighter crowns in heaven.

Sometimes in this busy world we temporarily forget who God is and insist on going according to our timing. He continuously reminds us that He doesn't work this way. Funny how God speaks to us through voice, word, and circumstances. We just have to learn to listen and then sit back and be amazed by Him. I know the difference of going through hard times not knowing the Lord and going through hard times knowing the Lord is on my side. I'm often guilty of slowing the peace process that comes from knowing God by spending time struggling with my human emotions.

Give Them Wings

I'm going to be a grandmother. Our daughter has persevered through many trials in her life and will be a wonderful mother because of God's early lessons. Together we will train and guide and help her child live life to its fullest. While our lives are being filled with responsibilities and surprises, we imagine Alexandra touching the hearts of everyone she meets.

How do grandparents please the Lord? By teaching their grandchildren from the very beginning who He is. Letting them know God is the best Father and Friend who will always love them, watch over them, and be at their sides. From my own experience I know a child's faith is shaped by imitating those closest to them. My husband and I are blessed with wonderful sons and good friends to help us to help our daughter in her baby's Christian growth. We will be a team to enrich Alexandra's knowledge of Jesus. She will be taught that prayers are always answered. Sometimes it comes as a quick yes or no. Sometimes God tells us to wait.

Grandparents teach your grandchildren that if they ask God to speak to them, He will. But, He may do it through the appearance of a beautiful rainbow or in the touch of a soft wiggly puppy. God's whispers may be heard in the song of a bird or the cries of a newborn baby. God may send a special friend, a guardian angel, to lift your grandchild's spirits when they are hurting. The important lesson to teach is to be ready with eyes and heart open to observe the little miracles happening around them.

Teach children that it is OK to believe in something they cannot see. Children can be taught to believe in Jesus as easily as believing in Santa Claus and the Easter Bunny. Children can love unconditionally without looking at color of skin or brand names on clothing. Jesus Loves the Little Children All the Children in the World: It is a parent's responsibility to teach the true meaning of these words and to put them into practice.

Just as easy as learning to love, a child can learn forgiveness and not to carry around destructive grudges. They can battle it out on the playground and be best buds in fewer than five minutes. A child can learn it's OK to need and ask for help. They can learn to seek out others who may be in need and reach out to them. A vital lesson for parents to learn is a child must know it's OK to laugh and to cry. God gave everyone the gift of laughter and tears to show emotions, when words don't work.

My daughter and I have seen many ways in which parents raise their children to know God. Some we agree with and some we don't. Some just don't appeal to us and some parents make us want to turn our backs and run as fast as we can in the opposite direction. We agree that a small child like Alexandra will have a healthy outlook on Biblical teachings if she is gradually fed simple things of the Bible and observes the goodness in those around her. I felt something missing in my life when I was growing up. I have hope Alexandra won't take as long as I did to have an intimate, up close, and personal relationship with God.

I'm disturbed when I see Christians raising their children in a way I feel is taking a different path than the one on which the Bible leads us. It is often difficult to hold my tongue and not judge. The truth that some parents find hard to accept is that God gave our children to us on loan and the quicker we embrace this truth the quicker we move on to what He has planned for our families. Our daughter believes in the Roots and Wings Theory. We teach our children to live God's way. We give them everything we can to help them grow strong- rooted in body and soul. Then we give them wings, freedom, to leave home and carry this knowledge to others. To want to hold on to our children and keep a small amount of control over them is probably the most natural need for loving parents. The Bible clearly states that if we raise our children this way, we did not do the job God assigned to us.

It was a difficult time in my life seeing my children move away. But it was also an exciting time to watch as they became new persons making plans for their future. I'm certain some of the sadness would have been lightened if I had understood the Roots and Wings Theory when they were toddlers and had prepared myself much sooner for an empty nest. It's a blessing to be asked to partner with my daughter in preparing her to give Alexandra room to fly.

The Bible repeatedly tells us that we come closer to Jesus through pain and mistakes. How does someone discover the person inside if they have nothing to compare with and nothing to test them? We will love Alexandra with an everlasting love. We will remind her that she might make mistakes, but she has our assurance that if she falls her family will be there to pick her up.

The words of a favorite Christmas song, *It Won't Be Long 'til Christmas*, written by Richard and Robert Sherman comes to mind as our adult children plan to spend the holidays at home this year. The song speaks of how quickly our children grow while we are busy guarding them the best we can. They soon fly away. The lyrics tell us that when we are saddened by their absence, we are to remember our children and the noise and laughter that once filled our home. Giving them space to grow and spread their wings will build their character and they too will miss the years past and will be home for Christmas.

Love

Jesus replied: Love the Lord with all your heart and with all your soul and with all your mind. This is the first
and greatest commandment. And the second is like it: Love your neighbor as yourself.
---Matthew 22:37-39

Three dear friends are going through hard times with loved ones. I was able to help Joan communicate with her adult daughter because of the trials my daughter and I have gone through. In Kathy's daughter-in-law I see myself. My mother-in-law loved me. She called me the daughter she never had and did everything on this planet to please me. I wasn't raised knowing how to love and what to do with love when it was given unconditionally. I continually pushed her away. Instead of putting a lump of coal in my Christmas stocking she filled it with love, which I wasted.

I see now that my mother-in-law tried to break the cycle of vices I'd grown up with and what had molded my personality at that point in my life. My mother-in-law tried to be nice to someone who didn't know how to be nice. Feeling abandoned by my mother after the adoption of my three sisters, was I afraid to let my mother- in-law love me? Afraid maybe, that she might also abandon me?

Elizabeth's problem is different from the other two. Her daughter is dying. Coming so close to losing my son after a doctor prescribed the wrong medication for asthma, I can embrace Elizabeth and tell her "I understand." We cannot fathom God's greatness and His plans for us. The reasons I missed out on the good times with my mother-in-law and able to use my mistakes to help my friends must be part of the big picture.

I studied the book of Job for a year with a gentleman whose intelligence far surpassed my own. Every third word he spoke I looked up in a dictionary. More time was spent with my nose in a dictionary than listening to God's Word. I studied Job again, but this time I did it my way. Each time I opened my Bible I asked God to help me read it, understand it, retain it, and apply it in my life. Summarizing the book in one sentence is to say, "I feel your pain." We have all heard people say, "I know how you feel". These people may be filled with compassion for the hurting, but how can one feel the pain without walking in that person's footsteps?

God certainly has allowed plenty of room in my life for mistakes and heart wrenching regrets. I can't say I enjoyed a minute of it, but I'm grateful when I can help someone by truly understanding their pain. We can never be more in Christ's image as when we reach out to meet the needs of others. Teach your children and grandchildren that God has a way of showing us the love we give away can come back to fill our hearts in amazing ways.

He Understands

The Lord searches every heart and understands every
motive behind the thoughts....
—1 Chronicles 28:9

It took me nine years to understand the purpose of writing my stories. I may still have gotten the answer wrong and if I did, I could live with it. When a friend read my first story, he commented he didn't know I could write. "I can't," I replied. "Every time I begin a new page, I ask God for the words to type." I hadn't yet gotten over allowing someone to read my manuscript, when I began another. Then I began questioning myself. "Am I pouring everything into something that does not fit into God's will?"

After several days with thoughts spinning out of control, knowing I've allowed myself to become transparent and there is no turning back,

I believe God intervened. He showed me I was still on the narrow path with Him with a daily devotional that came on my screen. The words "There are ways to be quietly with someone to let them know they're not alone in their pain," were just the words I needed to hear. I don't consider myself a speaker and when it comes to consoling another person in pain, I'm not gifted with beautiful words. In fact, three of my most loved friends have told me it took practice to be able to keep up with me when I speak. "Your conversations bounce around like a basketball," they said smiling.

Sitting in church one morning, I was looking forward to celebrating communion with my daughter and a dear friend sitting on the other side of me. I felt a change come over my friend and I reached over and held her hand for a moment. "I can't take part in communion this morning. I did something this week I'm ashamed of," she whispered. "What in the world did my sweet friend do?" I wondered. "Did you ask God to forgive you?" I asked. "Yes, I did, but I don't think He should because I haven't corrected what I did." I took her hand again. "If you have asked God to forgive you then He has." The sin is not accepting His forgiveness," I reassured her. The tray was nearing and she whispered, "You're right," as a look of peace came over her face. I did it. I had spoken to someone and had made sense. I didn't have to write something on paper and pass it to her.

Following church services that afternoon my friend called to say she had corrected her sin and felt much better. "I'll tell you what I did," she said sounding like a mischievous child getting caught with her hand in the cookie jar. "I let a sales-person ring up a sales price for an item that I knew wasn't on sale, but I returned it". I smiled imagining how the world would be if this were the level of sin we lived in.

Moses tried to use his speech impairment as an excuse not to do God's will, so his brother Aaron was designated by God to be his official spokesperson. It's a soothing thought that maybe God allows me to write for the same reason. Rambling usually describes my speech much more accurately than eloquent. Possibly by sharing my stories I can quietly help someone. The Bible clearly states we cannot be servants if we refuse to tell others about God, either with words or by our actions. It can also be a failure in God's eyes since sharing our faith may determine another's eternal mailing address.

It took a long time before I allowed myself to have fantasies of someone reading my material. We were created in the image of God and our purpose is to love others, but how do we obey this command if we don't have good thoughts about ourselves? I have never placed myself above another, but humility and pride did play a huge part in what I wanted others to know about me. Funny, since I started sharing who I really am my life has been filled with more peace than ever before.

Our Reward

The heavens declare the glory of God;
the skies proclaim the work of His hands.
—Psalms 19:1

Teach your children that if they set goals, God will supply them with the things they need to accomplish them. Learning to look at people's hearts and not their worldly possessions will be the most meaningful advice they hear. Some people may be very rich in money, but very poor in God's eyes. We want to teach Alexandra to glorify God in everything she does. We want her to know God is smiling as she puts her toys away and tells her mommy she loves her. Help to ingrain special scriptures on your children's hearts to sustain a gentle spirit and never doubt the abundant love surrounding them.

In the middle of last July, I sat on the back patio late in the evening with all the lights turned off. I stared up through a tall juniper tree and was fascinated by the arrangement of stars shining through the branches. It reminded me of lights on a Christmas tree. It wasn't long before I discovered it was the Big Dipper peeking through. The world has its problems, but when we stop long enough to smell the roses, we discover so many of God's masterpieces right under our noses, or over our heads.

I remember warm summer evenings long ago when I laid on the grass with my children watching the stars at night and playing the cloud game in daylight. I hope Alexandra will be able to flip the imaginary switch and turn off the hustle and bustle of this world when she feels the need. In doing so I've learned to rejoice in the quiet and embrace the beauty of God's unending tapestry.

An unusually chilly September morning finds me wrapped in an afghan, sitting in the garden with a mug of hot coffee. Even with a cold breeze, the smell of winter approaching, and the last lingering traces of summer and fall colors, this little piece of land God gave so graciously is magnificent. I have been reflecting on my regrets in life and how they have given me strength to face even bigger challenges. What will I tell Alexandra if she ask my advice on matters I have experienced firsthand? Will I be able to teach her that the first thing to grasp is an understanding that God knows what is best for all of us? God loves us. The Lord meets the needs of all Who love Him, but according to His will and in His timing, not ours. My mind zooms ahead to the future. It is never too soon to begin praying for Alexandra's teenage years and for her mother for any challenges they might face. A time when lessons in God's timing will be in great demand.

I want to teach my granddaughter to knit and crochet if her mother agrees. Hopefully she will never find it necessary to use this talent for the purpose I did. Instead of sitting in a dark room in a state of vegetation, I sought ways to keep my sanity in the mist of God's pruning and weeding in my life. I learned to crochet.

The children who had grown up in my California preschool had filled my life with a special gift. They gave me that childhood I never had and formed a security blanket around me. As soon as I finished one afghan, I began another and shipped them off to the California kids. Using 40 percent off coupons from Michael's to buy yarn, I must have made forty-five afghans in two months. I wonder how I might have responded to these dark times if my faith had been a slight measure of what it is today. Alexandra will know that loving Jesus brings greater rewards than making a hundred afghans!

Serenity

"God promises to give us our daily bread. He doesn't guarantee it will be buttered." I don't remember where I read these words, but what a statement to anyone believing the life of a Christian is easy. Every morning I start my day thanking God for His blessings and asking His forgiveness when I want more than what is being offered. I cannot ask for a better way to start my day than to know God is by my side to face each challenge the day might bring. It's OK to ask God to open the windows of heaven and let blessings stored up, rain down on us. Contentment and happiness complement each other. I still struggle with occasional envy of the material possessions of others and what I once had, though.

Greed is a sign of a person's emptiness and a fear he will never have enough to sustain him in life. He grabs onto everything in sight that's beneficial for himself. His victims are not his concern. Remembering people who have hurt me out of greed in the past fills me with sadness for them, not anger. When people "have it all,' what does that mean? Does it mean they have peace and security? Do they sleep well at night?

There are times I can't refrain from imagining our lifestyle if we had been more in tune to mankind's greed. Satan sure can pull some mighty tight rope when I picture being free of financial burdens, retired and driving across the country with that ready-packed pop-up-tent-trailer. God knew what He had to do to get our attention and it worked! This terrible defeat was a steppingstone in our spiritual growth. My time spent feeling disappointment has shortened considerably, yet, occasionally, a big disappointment comes along to test me.

Looking outdoors over manicured gardens of the beautiful home in which, we were invited to dinner, I wondered how I would ever be able to entertain this family in our tiny house. I asked God to forgive me for being envious. The following morning, I sat quietly in my purple chair, in my room, and I prayed. I thanked God for my beautiful little house and gardens. I thanked Him for the pruning and weeding He has done in my life to make me the person I am. I thanked Him for the relationship I have with my children and they with each other.

You might call it a revelation. God showed me something of greatness this morning. While I was preoccupied with envy of a family with material possessions, my family has shared a love for each other in past years this family lacks. I then found myself praying for the family. Teach your children that discouragement can turn into encouragement. Help them to understand that they will see fewer shadows if they look away from their disappointments in life and focus their eyes on Jesus. ***Enjoy what you have rather than desiring what you don't have. Just dreaming about nice things is meaningless; it is like chasing the wind. --- Ecclesiastes 6:9***

As a new grandmother I hope I have some of the answers to help my daughter, if she asks, to build self- esteem in Alexandra. Because I had no one to help me, I don't feel the confidence I want. I felt like a misfit growing up in my family and still do. It was not for the lack of money or a big house or any of those selfish things that made me feel like an outsider. Special ingredients that form a family unit were missing. No one took time to get to know the needs of each family member and spend time with them.

I have a very good memory of my childhood from early on. I can't remember being held or cuddled at any age. I can't remember being read to or tucked into bed at night. We never sat down together at mealtime like other families did or talk about the day's events. I once had a report card with all A's and B's except for the F in Spanish. No one glanced close enough to see that it had been changed to an A. My family lacked in structure and boundary-setting. There was no spiritual foundation to teach us how to love and be loved.

I remember something that happened in my preschool that may clarify my feelings of partial dysfunction. I had made pancakes for the preschoolers and after they poured the syrup, I sprinkled their pancakes with powdered sugar. As I was going through the line with the white powder, I heard the youngest of the group whisper in a frightened voice, "She's putting baby powder on our pancakes!" What if no one had been there to explain what the powder was and that there was nothing to fear?

There were times in my youth, even in high school, I imagined myself living in an orphanage without a family. I wondered what difference it would have made. In a classroom two years ago the unexpected happened. Our assignment was to bring a childhood snapshot of ourselves taken with our siblings. The picture I chose was a favorite, showing a little girl with big blue eyes and blonde hair. I never saw anything in it except that she was rather cute. The teacher asked us to hand the picture to the person on our left and describe what we saw in it. "I see three children," the lady said. "They are probably one, three, and ten. The three-year- old is smiling, but there is a look in her eyes of not belonging." I was that three-year-old.

By not having any sort of solid structure growing up, bits of dysfunction carried over into how I raised my children. I never really talked to them and they in turn never really talked to me about my feelings of insecurity.

Teaching the difference between righteousness and self-righteousness may be a good place to start when we talk to our children about self-esteem, which can also be defined as being self-conceited. Righteousness means a divine state of holiness or godliness and the credit for success is given to God. The Lord directs and redirects all the rewards and blessings in our lives. A self-righteous person takes credit or all the good that has been bestowed upon him. I've known a lot of people who have climbed the ladder of success and when they reached the top, they found themselves alone, without a true friend to pick them up if they fall. "Was it all worth it?" I've heard them ask.

Bedside salvation is an issue I have a problem accepting. How can a person live what some call the good life, which is only good for themselves, and on their death bed receive Christ and salvation? This was something I lifted to God right away instead of dwelling on it! I must remind myself that this is God's world, God's people, and Heaven is a gift from Him. Also, He is the only one who truly knows our hearts. Let us teach our children that there are no magic tricks to get into heaven.

In one incidence, self-righteousness was so deeply engrained in someone I knew personally that he went to his grave without a clue of the connection between his conceited heart and his fear of dying. "Until you have peace with God you will never find serenity within," is something this person never wanted to listen to. This person was a retired professional athlete. He had more money, benefits, fun times, and big toys than most of us can imagine having in a lifetime. One evening while having dinner in our home, I asked if a young boy's parents could bring their son over to meet him. The boy was an avid fan and had just come home from the hospital after being diagnosed with an incurable disease. I was stunned and ashamed when my friend replied, "I'd rather not, but here's an autographed game card. I really don't like doing those kinds of things. I like my privacy."

Desmond Tutu, in his book titled *God Has a Dream*, talks about generosity. He says, "Like humility, generosity comes from seeing that everything we have and everything we accomplish comes from God's grace and God's love for us." Even if it means taking time to shake a little boy's hand, we need to share God's gifts with others.

I thought about this last dinner we had together when reading a website devotional last week. A famous athlete was appearing at a publicity autograph signing for a group of children. Time to leave, children gone, no TV cameras. As the athlete's car was pulling away, he noticed a car drive up with a young boy wearing a sad face. The little fan was too late for the signing. The athlete turned the ignition off, got out of his car, introduced himself to the boy and gave him his autograph. This man will be welcomed at God's dinner table anytime, I'm sure. What's on the other side of death? Our Master is on the other side and when it's our time to go and we know our Father, we leave this world without fear. Instead we will be filled with gladness.

Relationships

The heartfelt counsel of a friend is as sweet
as perfume and incense.
---Proverbs 27:9

I spent yesterday with my friend Kirsten. We went all out for my birthday: After eating lunch at Taco Bell we shared a waffle bowl, hot fudge turtle sundae, topped with coffee bean sprinkles. When it comes to talking about heroes, I think of Kirsten as being a different kind of hero. She is one of my best friends, my sister in Christ, my sounding board and someone I can always depend on. She is the only friend who stayed with me as I struggled through my toughest trials after moving to Bend.

I went to bed last night thinking, who besides Kirsten and my late friend Charlie, do I call my hero? I have met countless women in Bend. Many were nice. An equal number were not so nice. Some women abandoned our friendship upon finding out my money was gone. Some of these women have lived through child molestation, being kidnapped, raped and beaten and left for dead. Some have been divorced and have seen their husbands marry the women with whom they were having affair. Someone has lost a child and the days for a second child are numbered. Still another has lost more financially from people she trusted than we have. Although the word "admiration" is appropriate, the title of hero doesn't fit everyone. Those women who have accepted Christ and have persevered and learned through their trials, those are people I call heroes.

Are you like millions of people in this world who own an address book? Every four or five years I buy a new one and by the time I delete the people I no longer have contact with, there are few names left to write in the new book. At first this makes me a little sad, but after a while the book begins to fill up again with people who bring new breath into my life. I've been in Bend for nine years and there have been a lot of names deleted from my old address book. Some of my greatest lessons, however, were learned through superficial friends. One thing I learned is that in a superficial relationship you can pretend to have it all together. Faking it won't work in a real relationship. The names I carry over to my new book I'm hoping will be around for a long time. I'm still growing in my faith and in myself, and I guess the old saying is true, "A friend will grow as you grow, or they will go."

Questions kept me awake for hours last night, but the outcome was well worth it. I thought of Fred Rodgers of *"Mr. Rodger's Neighborhood."* As a young mom I thought his ways were a little "foo foo." As an adult I saw this man wear his heart for children on the outside of his cardigan, and yes, I consider him a hero. At the top of my list of heroes are my husband and my daughter. My husband has supported me 100% in

The Walking Shoes

everything I've done for more than fifty years. Not an easy task for anyone to undertake.

I woke up this morning with my high-school class reunions on my mind. Drinking my morning coffee, brushing my teeth, standing under a hot shower, I couldn't get my ten-, twenty-, and thirty-year class reunions out of my head. "God, am I supposed to write about these reunions and how I was no more able to show the real me than when I was in school?" I asked. Committee meetings for all three reunions were held in my home, but the morning following each party I felt weird, as if I had been at the opening of a time vault that turned out to be a colossal disappointment. I plan not to attend the next one.

"OK God, if something is to come out of this, please spell it out for me." I know the first thing I'm expected to do is pray and keep my eyes open to listen for His instructions. The Holy Spirit gives us courage to stay rooted and to persevere. High school should have been a marvelous time for me. There were so many doors of opportunity opened up for me. I had offers to be in different circles of friends, from the popular groups to those in the bathroom where good girls never ventured. I was envious of girls who had best friends and when I was offered to join them, I didn't know how to accept the invitations.

I never felt normal in my relationships. There was so much I wanted to hide. Because I was one person on the outside, the one with no problems, and the me inside had absolutely no self-esteem and confidence or instruction on how to face any of this, I was constantly trying to prove to myself that I was that outside person. I detested who I was, both inside and out.

I left early this morning to give piano lessons and stopped on the way home to pick up shrubs to plant in the garden. The thought of writing about my class reunions hasn't left me. I have sad memories and don't know where to start and wonder if I can make any sense out of what I do write.

Another day has passed without writing and I believe yesterday was a chosen time from God to open my eyes to a few surprises. I wrote about always pretending I was someone else, always having a feeling of twenty people crowded into my body trying to please someone. I was surrounded by people who wanted to be my friend, but I felt alone. No matter my accomplishments, the class reunions made these old feelings of having to prove myself surface.

I may have entertained classmates in my home for the reunion meetings, and I may have laughed and danced along with everyone at the parties, but no one really knew who I was and I didn't know them. I couldn't understand those who had climbed the ladder of success and had gained new attitudes according to which rung they were presently standing on.

In my high school freshman year, I became friends with a boy I called Beaver. Because of my achievements in Algebra class, he called me Useless. My achievements by the way was nothing to brag about. I received an F after having the highest grade the first semester, keeping me from the honor roll the entire second semester. I wonder if our Algebra teacher would remember the day I wore my favorite blue corduroy jumper ordered from Seventeen Magazine, which crisscrossed several times in the back and tied in a bow.

When the bell rang Beaver smiled and said "See ya later." Sitting in an empty classroom, the only person left to untie me from my chair was the teacher who had a voice like a bear and was the size of the Jolly Green Giant. I exchanged warm greetings with Beaver at the ten and twenty-year-class-reunions. By the time our thirty-year-reunion rolled around; Beaver had become a highly successful Bay area Attorney. My old friend's new position on the social ladder and new attitude told me right away I'd be making a big mistake calling him Beaver.

What was missing in my life to cause these feelings of emptiness and detachment? I detest phony people. So why was I being one? My husband and I fell asleep after my last reunion around 2:00 a.m. after several hours listening to a loud argument coming from the adjacent room. We joked about putting a glass to the wall to see if we recognized the voices. At 2:15 a.m. I woke and wanted to go home. There was no need in continuing my game to be someone I'm not at a breakfast gathering.

Maybe seeing how a big title and prosperity had changed my friend Beaver was just what the doctor ordered. There were good people in that class and I take full blame for how I felt. I'd grown enough to know I no longer had to pretend to fit in but wasn't ready to be myself around them. My brain won't shut down thinking about my school days. One person takes center stage in all of this: a friend named Duffy. We started school together in kindergarten and graduated from eighth grade together nine years later. Duffy's parents watched over her homework and her grades. Her mother was a seamstress and Duffy had beautiful clothes. Most of mine were bad fitting hand-me-downs from a cousin. Her parents monitored her piano practice and I found myself wondering how it would feel to be on the receiving end of all that conventional stuff.

Duffy offered her expertise on how to dress and I accepted. She asked to meet me in the bathroom before class each morning in high school to style my long blonde hair. I held resentment for what she had and what I lacked. Of course, I didn't understand any of my feelings at the time. Looking back now, I'd say the word "insecure" best described me. She had it all and she wanted to be my best friend. Sad, yet true, we seldom appreciate what we have until we lose it. ***I thank my God every time I remember you. ---Philippians 1:3***

This afternoon while sitting on my patio, I thought about Duffy and how different my high school years might have been if we had stayed close through our senior year. She was popular, National Honor Society material, a cheerleader and had a large circle of friends. She always displayed confidence, something I wanted and could never imagine having. Silly to be admitting it decades later, but a pair of green tennis shoes ended that friendship. Duffy made a comment one day regarding my shoes. We both wore green tennis shoes that day. She commented how mine had rounded toes while hers were pointed. I knew mine came from Karl's Shoe Store and her shoes had come from Risutto's, the nice store across the street. I felt embarrassed. Instead of telling her, I walked away from a friend because of my own jealousy, envy, insecurity and I might as well add ignorance.

The memory I carry with me from the last class party I plan to attend, is sitting on the floor surrounded by friends from grade school Duffy, Patsy, Roman and Richard who were always my dates for Girl Scout activities. Duffy became a kindergarten teacher. I owned a preschool and was teaching piano. God sends people into our lives for a reason, a season, or a lifetime. I believe Duffy may have touched on each of these in my life.

I have explained how Kirsten became my first friend in Bend. She knew me when I had all the money and dreams, saw me through losing it, and stuck around to see me in God's arms today. Kirsten is always in a hurry, but when she asks, "How are you?" she's far from being done with you.

Showing yourself to a friend is easier said than done. For an authentic worth-saving friendship, you must have trust in that other person asking, "How are you?" and be honest when she sticks around to know the answer. If we're not honest, then there is no real friendship. Memories have a way of taking our minds in different directions. These school day memories recall people I haven't thought of for almost fifty years. When I was in fourth grade living in our rickety whitewashed house, a girl in sixth grade moved across the street with her large family into a barn. One summer we cleaned her outhouse, the only bathroom, and raked the loose dirt in the yard. She came up with an awesome idea. I would be a waitress in her hamburger café and kids would get off the school bus to be served burgers and fries. I don't remember what happened to change our dreams of serving hamburgers and fries and I never saw the friend after she moved to Arizona.

Wouldn't it be just like God to have fulfilled this girl's dream? What if God never allowed others to distract her from her dream? "Don't forget your dreams while living in God moment to moment. He will give to you everything you need to act on them," is a good lesson for any child to have engrained growing up.

Why the Children

I haven't taken a survey on what makes a good friend and a long-lasting relationship, but the idea sounds intriguing. What do you look for in a perennial friend? Someone who will always be there for you? Like the song says, "You just call out my name and I'll come running." I want my friend to be someone who loves me unconditionally and will be honest and tell me when I'm wrong even when I'm in denial.

I need a friend who will help build my confidence too. I've known a lot of people who tried, but I pushed them away in the same way I did Duffy, my grade-school friend. Pride prevailed, and my inside personality refused their help, causing the meek person inside to withdraw even more. The question has been asked, "If salvation is our only purpose on this earth, then what do we do until we go to heaven?"

God created us for a purpose in this world and the Bible tells us heaven will wait. Helping others build confidence to face troubles in this mixed-up world can take our minds off our own worries and sometimes the travails diminish in the process. There is a lot of truth in the saying, "It is better to give than to receive." God placed us here not to think only of ourselves, but to help others. I believe that refusing help is as much a sin as not offering it.

My advice to anyone setting out to write for the first time is to have a completely unbiased stranger critique your work. As for me, I listened to praises from friends who knew me and had already gained insight into whom I am. I became stuck without direction to pull myself out. Then a completely unbiased stranger read the first story I wrote. I was hurt and shocked, even embarrassed, by his comments. The pages seemed to have been chewed up and spit out. I felt my stomach turn inside out and the hot flashes I'd been fortunate to avoid hit with full vengeance. I felt a fool for thinking I had talent for writing. I felt an idiot to have allowed my writing to go beyond my safety zone and the manila envelope.

An hour later, after a third or fourth time reading through his critique letter filled with questions and comments, I began realizing what an amazing favor this man had done. I immediately e-mailed to thank him for being a friend who opened my senses to the new roads to take my writing. What interested him the most as a reader were my omissions, those I thought I could keep buried. Oh, I could write some juicy stories for readers to jump right into. Stories that would hold a reader's interest, giving certain clarity to questions remaining after reading a story such as mine. Stories that would leave a reader wanting more. But I've been trusted not to repeat these stories. "Are you doing this to glorify Me or yourself?" I have heard when struggling to honor this. So, my omissions stay as they belong--untold.

What really made me angry was his observation that I seemed happy only when taking care of children. Lo and behold, the man is right. And why shouldn't I have been the happiest when working with these kids? The gentleman asked if I had some control issues. It's possible, but nothing I ever thought about and doubt if any of the children did either. It would be interesting to know if they did.

Dogs and children are some of the most magnificent creations made by God. If we only allow them, they will love us unconditionally and bring joy into our lives when others can't. My children get more of this love from me than I did from my parents. My wish is that each of us learns from the previous generation and carries something positive into the next. My granddaughter is well on her way to receiving an abundance of what a child needs growing up because of the children I've helped raise.

I've received reminders through the years of how God uses everyone and everything to build our confidence and trust in Him. A wonderful group of kids went through my preschool and music lessons. I pulled out a three-year-old letter today from a young woman who had just been accepted to medical school. Weeda is a nickname given by the older preschoolers when my name was difficult to pronounce by some of the younger ones and it seems to have stuck.

> "Weeda,
>
> Well if you needed a Kleenex for the thank you note, then you will definitely need one for the personal statement I wrote. For my application I had to write three short essays, two having topics and one being open ended. So, for the open ended one I wrote about you and how your influence allowed me to be the student I am. Here it is:
>
> My hands glide across the black and white keys and an endless stream of notes are all I see. The sweet sound of the piano fills the air and my mind relaxes. The rhythm of the music and the smooth beat brings back memories of my childhood, where the world was

so fresh and new. I close my eyes and see myself, not as a young woman with my future awaiting me, but with a young mind, with the world ahead of me. The loving face of Juanita makes my fingers hit the right notes and reminds me of all the little things she has taught me; and how those little things turned into something big.

Juanita was not only my piano teacher; she was my friend, my educator, my inspiration, and my mentor. When I was only four years old, Juanita opened my eyes to a world of color, music, reading, and numbers. Her unique methods and personal touch accompanied each lesson which made learning easy and something each child was eager to do. Songs, sign language, traveling, and dressing up made education come to life and diversified my experiences at a young age. With Juanita's influences, my education started off on the right foot, and allowed me to experience education as a journey, exploring new dimensions each day. As time progressed, my days with Juanita as a teacher became more and more distant. Preschool was over, and I no longer had childlike thoughts, but was ready to use the resources that she shared with me. Throughout school, although I did not see it, Juanita was there every step of the way.

Because of her teachings, when difficult ideas were put in front of me, I automatically rose to the challenge. Instinctively, the unknown was seen as a good thing, and I was not hesitant to tackle it. With her preparation, my skills and ability to grasp new concepts allowed me to excel quickly; it was as if I was conditioned for the great race in front of me. Now when I am faced with long calculus problems, detailed research papers, and confusing scientific equations, they are all seen as obstacles I can overcome. The facts and understandings from the projects have stayed with me just as the piano keys and notes did when I was in preschool. My desire to learn has stayed close at hand over the years and has allowed me to receive straight A's since the third grade. School is a part of my life that is challenging work but is something that I enjoy.

With Juanita's influence, academics have become a top priority and she continues to inspire me to learn new philosophies. When I am on my own in college, I will come across different methods of learning; however, the building blocks that she created will always be the foundation of my education. As these memories dwindle, I open my eyes and realize that my hands are still moving up and down the smooth keys. After thinking of my past, my fears and insecurities about my future have disappeared like the sounds of the piano. I look over my shoulder and search for Juanita, and although she is not there, I can still see her caring face. I am grateful that she planted the seeds of learning when I was so young, because now my roots are strong. My future awaits me, and I start a new chapter in my life. I know with my deep roots, I will be able to grow and turn into the person Juanita knew I would be.

I just want to tell you that I meant every word of it. I could never thank you enough for all that you taught me. Not only about school, but about life in general. Your hospitality and influence will always be with me, even though the difficulty of college. I have nothing but wonderful memories about the years we spent with you and I will never forget them.

I love you Weeda!"
Michelle

A note came from the parents of another preschooler not far behind this one. Two years following my move to Oregon I received an audio tape in the mail of Lauren playing piano. "I know, I know. You said if I just practiced I'd be fantastic," she said in her usual confident voice at the end of the tape. I received an e-mail when she was twelve and spending the summer in Europe: "The best times in my life were spent with you," it read.

The same little six-year-old who laid her head on my shoulder and yawned because she was bored in the middle of her very first piano lesson and didn't return for six months, is entering her third year in a prestigious school of music. This young woman who has become an outstanding musician is also studying in the field of music therapy. I received the following note from her parents.

"Dear Weed,

I cannot tell you in words how well our daughter plays the piano. We also want to tell you she is studying to become a collaborative accompaniment—where she is being trained to accompany singers for auditions—mostly operative arias. She has to play as well as be able to coach the singer on diction (Italian, French, and German) and pitch. It all started with M&M's on the piano keys and your patience."

Yes, God often sends messages, reminding us of how He uses everything and everyone to build our confidence and our trust in Him. Parents tend to have high expectations and busy schedules, due either to their own desires or that of the economy, and sometimes don't realize how quickly children grow up. I know I didn't. God is the Rock, but isn't it nice to think of us adults as being His helpers, the pebbles He places around the children?

A True Friend

*Share each other's troubles and problems,
and in a way obey the law of Christ.
If you think you are too important*

> *to help someone in need, you are only fooling yourself. You are really a nobody.*
> *---Galatians 6:2-3*

My Bible class meets every Friday afternoon. Someone usually finds encouragement from the group to see them over a hard spot. In moments of loneliness, and we all have them, the best thing we can do is to invite a friend to share our pain, even if it means sitting beside each other and saying nothing at all. These Friday Ladies are the best cheerleaders a person can ever hope for. Without experiencing failure, discouragement, and pain, we would not probe for improvements in our lives. I believe God gave us the gift of friends to make our pathway to Him a little smoother and less desolate.

I talk a lot about long-lasting friends, I guess because I've never had one. Even now, with so many good people in my life who I call friends, there is a tendency to wonder how long they will be around. I'm positive the stranger was right when he said I probably set myself up for disappointment by pouring everything I have to give into a relationship. Maybe my expectations of a friend are set too high.

I want my friend to defend me when I'm right, forgive me when I make a mistake, and be reliable when I'm in trouble. It took a devastating wrongdoing by a group of people for me to fully understand the difference between true friends and superficial ones. Let us teach our children that having one true friend is much more meaningful than having an abundance of superficial friends who cling to you for personal gain and turn their backs when you have nothing left to offer.

A true friend will not betray my trust. In Bible class last week, we discussed what God is speaking about when He talks in parables regarding a sower of seeds, weeds, tares, field and harvesters. God is the gardener who sowed us, whom He refers to as the seeds, into the world which is the field. Seeds are the righteous and sinners He calls the tares or weeds. The angels are the harvesters who will separate the nonbelievers from believers when Christ returns to take His children home.

It took months to understand that a parable is a short story taken from daily life to teach of salvation and heaven. It took even longer

The Walking Shoes

to understand what I first thought was gibberish. It took even longer to know "Being thirsty for the Word," wasn't just a bunch of mumbo jumbo slang. For weeks I was too embarrassed to ask what people meant by "the Word." An immense amount of perseverance was necessary to stick with my studies and learn from asking questions. Embarrassment went out the window when I became a witness to the miraculous way the Bible speaks to each of us and I am convinced there are no wrong questions.

A friend must be someone with whom I can vent raw anger with and with whom I can get up close and personal. The first person who comes to mind is my husband. If I can't let it all out to my best friend and partner in life, then something must be missing in our marriage. The Bible speaks about being unevenly yoked. I don't believe in horoscopes but find them amusing from time to time because they often hit close to home. According to most horoscopes, a Libra and a Scorpio are opposites and the most illogical people to cross paths. Yes, that's us. I'm the Libra and my husband is a Scorpio, who share few common interests, and I'm the first to say this has not been easy on either of us.

My husband and I fit our projected profiles. He is an Italian with a quick temper, although it has mellowed tremendously through the years. I'm the opposite. He raises his voice, nothing more, and that's when I have to remind myself how much I love him and it's OK not to like him at that moment. There were many times in our early years of marriage I chose to hold in my anger. I felt like calling him names and throwing something when he failed to read my mind. I chose to give him the silent treatment instead. Bad mistake. Worst mistake a wife can make. "Something wrong?" "No." "What's wrong?" "Nothing". "Have I done something to upset you?" "No." "Are you mad at me for something?" "No." What did I gain from the silent treatment? Absolutely nothing more than frustration and distance in our relationship.

I have vital information for all brides: Do not assume that your new husband knows what he is doing or what he is supposed to do. He usually doesn't any more than you do. Also, don't expect him to be a mind reader! It took most of our forty-eight years of marriage to resolve this problem. If you want him to do something ask him. It's that simple. When I was pregnant, there were times I cried because I wanted my husband to touch my stomach and feel the baby kick. I never asked him, thinking if he wanted to he would. It wasn't until our daughter asked her father to touch her stomach and feel the baby kick that I had the opportunity to share my secret. I reminded him we were very young and filled with false expectations of how marriage was supposed to come automatically perfect.

Don't get angry because your husband hasn't taken out the garbage and you have to do it yourself. Ask him to do it. If he refuses, let him know how you feel! If he still refuses, then find out what is missing in your marriage. Another piece of advice, and possibly one of the most important, is never, never, substitute milk with baby formula in your husband's mashed potatoes! Besides never letting you forget, you may have to clean up the mess as I did, after the first shocked mouthful flew across the kitchen table. My husband had a sweet tradition of apologizing. Every time he raised his voice and stormed out the front door, he returned with a smile and goodies from the local bakery. My much older and much more rounded body is grateful that he no longer feels the need to make bakery runs.

God hands out trials and sometimes they come in the form of a mate with whom you share limited interests, who in the past has made you want to pull your hair out, but you still want to be with no one else. I love my husband dearly, but there have been times I've asked God to let me be in love with him again. Last night, assuming I was asleep, he tenderly picked up my hand and kissed it, then gently laid it back down. I stayed very still, not wanting to lose the moment of knowing how much I am in love with my husband.

I have my personal opinions of companies advertising to match you with the "Perfect Person." We need to teach our children scripture that tell us not to search for that special mate. God will send him. We know God doesn't make mistakes and maybe He presents situations to see how hard we will work to love someone He has chosen for us. Too often people give up on relationships and marriage because, surprisingly enough, it really is hard work.

I need a friend who is not a gossip. A gossip is someone who says what someone else wants to hear and goes to the next person and does the same to be accepted. This trait is not acceptable in my perfect friend. Teach your children and grandchildren at a very young age that gossiping and being a busybody can be hurtful. The results usually include being hurt yourself and the loss of someone who God may have sent to become a true friend.

I want a friend who, just by being with me, brings strength, endurance, healing, and hope. Faithfulness builds security. A friend will comfort me when I'm hurting. My friend will reach out to others for fellowship and stand firm in their own faith. Someone who is lukewarm won't fit the qualifications of my perfect friend. We need to discourage our children from spending time with people who continually disappoint them, break their promises, stomp on their dreams, are too judgmental and have different values and any friend who runs away during difficult times. This is not a friend.

A gusty wind created a rustling sound through the aspen branches as I waited for the storm to blow in. Stars shot across the sky. Soon thunder beat like drums and sheets of lightning flashed. Before deciding it was time to move indoors, I spent time thinking about my perfect friend. There have been a lot of people who have passed through my life. Some were good, and some were bad. Some filled many of my qualifications and some never came close. There is only one perfect friend: Jesus. Teach your children to have no misconception about this truth.

So Little Time

Whatever is has already been, and what will be has been before; and God will call the past to account.
—Ecclesiastes 3:15

"If I could save time in a bottle," are words from the song, Time in a Bottle, written by the late Jim Croce. "But there never seems to be enough time to do the things you want to do once you find them."

I would love to see the number of hands raised in a large room where the audience has been asked, "Who would like to see the hands of time turned back for just one day?" and told to "Make a list of changes you would make from your past." These words from Jim Croce's song, pretty much sum up my thoughts about reaching back in time. We search for those special things that make us happy and then we run out of time to enjoy them. Sometimes we had them in our back pocket all along, but just didn't know it. I speak for myself from experience. My pockets were filled many times over, but I had no idea.

My prayer is for our children and grandchildren to live life to their fullest, so they will not want to turn back time to erase hurts or feel the need to fill empty places. I know with God as our guide, we can all be a part in giving this prodigious gift to the young people around us.

What triggered the thoughts running through my mind this morning? Were they there when I fell asleep last night? Did I dream them? Or are they changes I would make if I could turn back the hands of time and live my life over? With God's help, heart wrenching regrets have become only bad memories. Bad memories, like regrets, can take our eyes off Jesus. We must surrender them to Him and ask that He continue to open our eyes that we can see the truth that sets us free.

There are so many beautiful old hymns we sing in church. "Turn your eyes upon Jesus, look full in His wonderful face…And the things of earth will grow strangely dim in the light of His glory and grace," is a favorite. I once read, "Don't let shadows of yesterday ruin your today." Such a powerful sentence to engrain in the minds of our children, along with the words from this song.

When was the last time you did something really dumb like placing a pot of hot coffee in the refrigerator, or pick up one of your children from school leaving the other stranded? How about sitting on an exercise bike thinking "I sure hope I'm in shape when I die and can fit into some nice clothes hanging in my closet that I haven't been able to wear in a while." Yes, I actually caught myself thinking this the other day. I could probably write a quick book of my most embarrassing moments and how family and friends find them ridiculously funny.

One night after an exercise class with friends, I made a comment they are still laughing at thirty years later. I shared with them for the first time that I never go to bed without the dishes being done and the kitchen cleaned, in case someone breaks in.

God once visited two sisters on His way to Jerusalem. While Mary sat at Jesus' feet listening to Him speak, Martha busied herself with cleaning and preparing dinner. I once was Martha, no doubt about it. Happy to say I'm more like Mary now, although I have found myself holding on to a few of Martha's housekeeping hints. How sad to look back at the amount of time I put into cleaning rather than playing with my children. My house will stay clean and tidy for my grandchildren, but there will be more time spent playing

I've learned we have been given the honor of teaching our children that God wants them to embrace His creations, work hard and manage their resources, in order to glorify Him. I will give it my best shot to help my grandchildren learn to offer love, understanding, and support to everyone they meet, traits I was never taught. We are to teach our children to understand they are worthy enough to receive these things from others as well. I was offered special gifts and I didn't know how to accept them. It is important to teach our children to love themselves and take risks, which is not the way some of us were brought up. I'm sure most kids are not mature enough to think "What's in that person's heart? What troubles are they carrying with them?" Instead of making judgments on what they see, I hope our children look at a person's heart.

As our children grow, they will find life to be an obstacle course, with troubles either for themselves or loved ones lurking around every turn. If my grandchildren pay attention to nothing else, I ask that they remember God blesses us when we hold up under troubles. It's a difficult thing knowing our children will someday face troubling times. What can we do to help them avoid the detours?" is the first thought for most parents and grandparents. Each of us has to choose how we respond to pain and hardships.

The Bible is filled with bitter sweetness. There are words to make us happy and sad. Words for brightening our day or to bring gloom. In our weakest moments God can send just the right scripture to do His greatest work in us by strengthening us. The Bible, God's bar of soap, as it's been called is our guide to understanding life and the how to of partnering up with God to transform this world before His return. Let us instill in our children the importance of knowing and understanding this book. By doing this, our children will know that forgiveness allows us to see obstacles blocking us from receiving serenity within and by removing them, clear the way for all sorts of good things to happen.

Sitting at my computer at 11:30 p.m. last night, I was listening to an oldies channel. "The mountain is high and the valley so low, can't seem to get to the other side," I hadn't heard that song in decades. Isn't this a place we all experience at least once in our lifetimes? "You just call out my name and wherever I am I'll come running to see you again. You've got a friend." Jesus is a friend we never have to look for or second-guess motives. Let us teach the children to know Jesus is just waiting for them to call Him.

Earl Grant's At The End Of A Rainbow was the evening's finale. 'At the end of a river the water stops its flow. At the end of a highway, there's no place you can go. Our love will go on until the end of time." WOW! This beautiful song gave me goose bumps. Our children must know that there is one love that will go past the end of time, though. Our Father in heaven will love us for eternity. *For as high as the heavens are above the earth, so great is His love for those who fear Him; as far as the east is from the west, so far has He removed our transgressions from us. ---Psalms 103:11-12*

What changes will I make as a grandmother, for my grandchildren, now that I'm grown up and have been on the battlefields and persevered? I will take advantage of the second chance God has given me to be the mother I wanted to be for my children and the grandmother I wished to have for my own children.

If my grandchildren invite me to take dance classes in college years and 6 a.m. aerobic classes like their Uncle Eric did, I won't just squeeze time into my schedule to do it. I will make the time to do it. If they want to learn cross-country skiing with me like their Uncle Michael did, I will do it. I don't want to feel too old to play like a kid. The best part in all this is that my daughter, who doesn't appreciate the beauty of snow country, will be playing alongside of us. The time lost with my children is irreclaimable. The time to create memories for them when I'm gone is now.

In His Time

A time to scatter stones and a time to gather stones.
A time to embrace and a time to turn away. A time to search
and a time to lose.
A time to keep and a time to throw away.
---Ecclesiastes 3:5-6

Too often we don't realize what a small act of kindness can do. Things as simple as a touch, a smile, a kind word, or a compliment, are small acts of caring that have the potential to bring joy into someone's life. God places people in our lives for a reason, a season, or a lifetime. Embrace them all.

A pastor spoke a few Sundays ago on what God thinks of religion. His father was an assistant pastor. This Bend pastor went to church his whole life and hated it. Hippies had moved into the little town where he lived, but never stepped foot inside the church. "I know they would have been asked to leave if they had entered," Pastor said. In his early twenties he attended one of the largest Christian churches in Oregon, a church in his hometown that was formed by the same group of hippies and is now staffed by their children and grandchildren. Living proof of God's invitation to everyone to take refuge in Him not just those dressed in their Sunday best, smelling good with clean untangled hair, and wearing shoes, but everyone!

I once attended a church that in all its years never had a Christmas tree. The pastor thought it was a bad thing. Christmas Eve services were never held. The pastor thought it was not necessary. No one shared their own opinions and needs. I suppose I'm a rabble rouser. I asked the new pastor's permission to have a Christmas tree. "We can also have Christmas Eve services," he added.

Longtime members ignored the tree standing at the front entrance of the fellowship hall saying, "A tree inside a church is not Christian." It did put smiles on the faces of newer members like myself. Pastor moved the tree inside the sanctuary on his own accord. Twinkling lights on a tree decorated with angels, the smell of fresh pine, and the sound of

Christmas carols being sung to glorify God, were a long time coming. I read a beautiful quote last year by Helen Keller, in a book called *A Family Christmas:* "The only blind person at Christmas is he who does not have Christmas in his heart."

I for one know Jesus was smiling on us that morning, although the choir complained they had difficulty singing with the tree staring at them. God wants His children to love others as we want to be loved. God wants us to toss religion out the window. I believe God wants us to find a home in church where we can live by faith, not by rules, regulations and traditions, or a one-person rule. These four things have a tendency towards bashing other churches and other church members. I'm visualizing a beautiful picture of my granddaughter's first Christmas Eve. Wiggling in church, dressed in red velvet, loved ones surrounding her and twinkling lights reflecting in big beautiful dark eyes like her mother's.

There are verses in the Bible I'm not printing because I don't understand them fully. Jeremiah Chapter 10 speaks about idolatry bringing destruction. It speaks about people cutting down a tree, decorating it with silver and gold and using it as an idol. Like anything else, good can be turned to evil and I agree that the true meaning of Christmas has been kicked around and tossed aside for years.

Teach your children and grandchildren that the true meaning of the birth of Christ is the joy of giving thoughtful gifts to people you love and those less fortunate than you. Show them that a gift of giving doesn't have to be wrapped in pretty paper and ribbon. Teach your children as we plan to teach Alexandra, that in giving to people who don't know Christ, there is a chance they soon will look for Him. Pray that our children will learn at a young age the joy one gets when giving from the heart.

How much more testing will God do before it's all over? Sometimes I end my prayers by asking this question. I usually put in my two cents worth about how wonderful it will be when the testing is done, when there is no reason to ask for forgiveness, and our want list for help is no longer necessary. I don't dare ask God for patience to wait it out. Patience can sometimes be our worst enemy. As difficult as it is to believe when we see our world crumbling, God does make everything beautiful in His time. This is a time we really have to pour out our trust in the Lord and accept the unknown as a child. During our testing God continuously gives us opportunity to pass. He has many testing techniques. He stretches us and gives pop quizzes. God also gives open book tests and repeat exams until we pass! This is my kind of teacher.

We received a newsletter from our homeowner's association asking us not to put coffee grounds down the garbage disposal, because it can ruin the sewage lines. I've always put my coffee grounds down the disposal. One morning, soon after my baptism, with coffee filter tipped almost upside down in the sink, I remembered the newsletter. I tried to dump the grounds thinking "This is silly, it won't harm anything," but my hand wouldn't move. I haven't tried since. Alexandra, I will tell you the story of how the Holy Spirit refused to let Nonny dump coffee grounds down the disposal and how He will help you win victory over temptation in the tiniest of circumstances.

The longer we read about God and the longer we talk to Him and learn to be still and listen to Him, the stronger we grow in our faith. The more mature we become, the more powerfully the Holy Spirit will convince us to do right. When there is a deep restlessness inside us, you can bet God is trying to tell us something. We may try to take our minds in another direction, but that stirring in our soul remains. Many times, I have felt this deep restlessness. The major changes I've made each time in my life, because of these feelings, always brought me into a place surrounded by children. Not knowing God personally, I never put the two, my love of working with kids and God, together until now.

Because I am reflecting on restlessness, let's talk about church hopping. A slang phrase, but not a bad description, at least in my way of viewing it. Some people look down on those who go from church to church looking for the right one. Please note that I didn't say the perfect church. Looking for the perfect church can take us down the wrong path, and I've traveled it before. I've finally learned to rely on the Holy Spirit to guide me in my search. I'd been content going to the new church until last week. Every Sunday I went alone, and I listened to a wonderful sermon by a great speaker. I had decided after my first visit that it was OK if no one came up to say hello or goodbye, because it's such a big church.

Last Sunday the pastor gave his usual wonderful sermon, but I felt alone and sad. Two days prior I had spent with my Friday Ladies Bible group. On Saturday I enjoyed my daughter's baby shower with the same group of people. Sunday at church I felt a restlessness that stayed with me until we met at Doris's house for a potluck.

This morning I tested my restlessness. My friend and neighbor, Gigi, went with me to Doris's church. The sermon was powerful, and the music was beautiful. There was no restless feeling or a feeling of being alone. I go to church to hear God's word, but I also love the comfort of loved ones to lean on.

Every breath we take, every move we make, every thought we have is in God's plan. Can God be allowing time to test ourselves to see how much we have grown, and will He soon send a reminder that He does make everything beautiful in His time?

When We Get To Heaven

And since I, the Lord and Teacher have washed your feet, you ought to wash each other's feet. I have given you an example to follow. Do as I have done to you. How true it is that a servant is not greater than his master. Nor are messengers more important than the one who sent them. You know these things—now do them! That is the path of blessing.
--John 13:14-17

Have you wondered what you will be doing in heaven? Being the busy person, I am, I'd like to think we won't be those heavenly angels floating around on clouds snacking on bagels and cream cheese. If I could pre-register for heavenly jobs, I'd sign up to be in the heavenly chorus (of course in heaven we never sing off tune). I would also ask to help with the gardening (which in heaven means no weeds). Let us have a mindset that joy comes from giving, not in the returns. Look at yourself as a servant not the one to be served. I looked up the meaning of 'giving' just now. Webster's Dictionary defines it as to bestow without a return, which I interpret as being a servant!

When I think of angels I am in awe of their purpose here on earth. I can grab an armful of books and search scripture for proof of their being, but why should I? I believe God has assigned a guardian angel to each of us and has given us free will to accept the angelic help or ignore it. And I believe my grandchild's guardian angel will be with her from birth.

I'm a steadfast believer that everyone is given the opportunity to become an angel, if we allow God's spirit to use us. Maybe we aren't the angelic kind, but what if we are given special gifts to assist the angelic angels? Pretty awesome to think of myself working in partnership with a guardian angel. Have you ever reached out and purposely touched someone and thought of angel wings brushing us in the same way? Have you ever smiled at a stranger and suddenly see a wrinkle fade? How many times has someone smiled at you in passing for no apparent reason and it made your own face shine? When is the last time you offered kind words to someone in pain and wondered how many times an angel has done this for you?

A guardian angel's hand can reach out and save us. So many times, I know this has happened for me and my family. A guardian angel must have been there when I pulled my car off the tracks just in time for the speeding train to pass by. An angel must have been with my daughter when she was minutes from drowning. Many times, I believe my family has been protected from danger. God gave us eyes to see and ears to hear. By using these gifts respectfully, we gain more awareness of what happens around us.

I admit to being human. There are times when smiling and reaching out to someone who looks and dresses like me is easier than doing the same for someone with a dirty face, grubby clothes, or tartar on their few existing teeth. I'm still one of God's works in training and I'm learning to bypass what I may see on the outside and search for what wonderful stuff might be buried underneath. What better way to understand the often-asked question, "Why do we exist?" We pray that Alexandra will keep her heart open to the needs of others.

The noise of the garden sprinklers awakened me a 5:30 a.m. The last question on my mind before falling asleep still lingers: "How does God work in our lives when we feel downcast and we take our eyes off of Him?"

Wonder Woman, Super Mom, Wife, Friend....Helppppppp! I hadn't felt like that in a long time. Then one Sunday, not long ago, it happened! We came home from church. My daughter was at work. My husband made a run to the grocery store. I made my dish for the monthly potluck at Jim and Doris's and cleaned the kitchen. Collapsing in the computer chair in a quiet house, which is a rare occurrence, I began writing. "Do you want coffee?" My husband asked quite sweetly when he walked in. "Sure," I said, but he was really asking if I'd make the coffee. There was a bowling tournament he didn't want to miss on TV. I made the coffee and quickly sat down again to write. I remembered I hadn't made the extra dish for my elderly friend, who is vegetarian and was planning to join us for the potluck.

Rushed for time now and a little warm under the collar, I went into my clean kitchen, prepared the vegetarian dish and cleaned the kitchen once more. Walking back to my computer I yelled as my husband sat down in my chair because of the sudden mental picture I had of him deleting the last ninety-minutes' worth of writing. After all that my vegetarian friend didn't show for the potluck. ***If you want to be great in God's Kingdom, learn to be a servant to all,***" I said as I asked forgiveness for my thoughts. Another one of those hymns that say a lot in just a few words.

I guess I should add Super Servant to my list of Wanna-Be's. A lesson to teach our children and grandchildren is that God doesn't expect us to take on every responsibility. Not only does it take our time away from Him, it takes responsibility away from someone who may be better qualified to fill God's will. Learn to set boundaries. Don't wear yourself out being both Mary and Martha.

White stock, orange poppies, Shasta daisies, and purple coneflowers, amongst other brilliantly colored blooms, were coming together like a rainbow outside our bedroom window. We'd had colder than usual days for September in Central Oregon. I expected to see the garden shutting down under the stress of frost, but there are new flowers popping up and others coming into a second bloom. Amazing how we cultivate and tend the soil and then watch as it turns into something beautiful for the eyes to behold. Instead of giving up in bad weather the garden is reborn. I watch in amazement as God cultivates and tends my family and when we struggle through the storms, He turns us into something beautiful in His eyes. We can now see where God is in all this.

My husband walked in as I stood in front of the bedroom mirror this morning with mascara in hand. He showed me a picture of a music box he wants to get his grandchild for her first Christmas. The top looks like a letter addressed to Granddaughter. When opened the box plays You Are So Beautiful. It is inscribed with a blessing telling Alexandra how much she is loved. Papa is in love with a baby he hasn't met. Sunday morning tears? Geesh! This usually happens at church, not before even leaving the house.

I was surprised when my husband was ready to leave for the new church a second Sunday in a row. He sat in a relaxed position with no frown on his face. At one point he actually uncrossed his stiff arms and laid his hands in his lap. When you know someone's body language as well as I know my husband's you don't miss a move. The longer my husband and I are together, the clearer it is to see that to grow old together is a blessing.

The pastor's sermon focused on worshiping one God. "We are not to criticize another's style of worshiping, but learn to accept it," he said. "The only wall that stands between those believing in the same God are those not believing Jesus was the Son of God who died on the cross for our sins." Of all the sermons Pastor had to choose from today, this is the one I wanted my husband to hear. My family believes that people may see, or hear, or touch, or smell the same things, but it can be different for each of us. If my husband had stood up to sing, I would have passed out right there on the spot.

Through Alexandra's Eyes

We will not hide these truths from our children but will
tell the next generation about the glorious deed of the
Lord. We will tell of His power and the mighty miracles He did.
--Psalms 78:4

Alexandra, my grandchild, your arrival will be the greatest thing to happen in our family since your mother and uncles were born. Maybe your arrival will bring even more blessings with it because you will be the cord that pulls us closer together. There are so many things I pray for you. Watching your mother anxiously waiting and preparing for you for nine months, and knowing God wrote the story of you, is a miracle.

I've known from the moment God answered my prayer for a grandchild, that He has a special purpose for your life. I prayed that same prayer for a grandchild for years, but now realize the hardships you might have suffered because our family was not ready for you. We are definitely ready, willing and able to take you on the magnificent journey God has prepared for you.

A multitude of obstacles blinded me from seeing the needs of my children. These same obstacles made it impossible to look ahead and plan for their future. God uses everything and every experience in our lives to let us reach out and touch someone. My own experiences will let me reach out and touch you. There are no obstacles blinding me to what you need from a grandmother and what God wants for your future. I am also here for your mother when she needs a helping hand.

Alexandra, I pray for your eyes to be open to all of God's creation. Become confident in your own life so you can share happiness with others. Take risks sooner than I did. Search for the talents God gives you and thank Him for His gifts. Quitting my job as a dental technician to teach piano, knowing only the right-hand staff notes, and opening a preschool, all came from taking risks. Writing when I've had no proper training also comes from taking risks.

A thought came to me today as I polished the silver coffee and tea set. I once had plans for the special group of boys and girls I left in California to come each summer and visit me. Living next door to tennis courts, another reason I chose that particular hilltop property, I had plans for hiring a tennis coach for them. I planned days of water rafting and biking. I planned reunions in the big house with these kids and their families. So many plans that never developed because of difficult times I chose not to share with them. A small part of my dream was to serve Baby Sara, Michelle, Lisa, Kathryn, Lauren, and Jessica hot cocoa from the silver tea set that had never been used in all the years of sitting in our home. This dream never came true for them, but it will for you Alexandra. One day you will look upon the tea set and remember our special times with a smile on your face and a story to tell your little girl.

I will watch you pray everyday Alexandra. With your eyes open to the troubles of this world, I want you to witness the power of prayer and see the amazing things that happen when God hears your voice. I ask for many wonderful gifts for you as you grow from a newborn baby into a beautiful young woman. Passion for other people and enthusiasm to learn take priority on my list, but there is much more I ask God to give you. I ask that curiosity keep your mind fresh and alive. I want you to be able to embrace new ideas and be ready for changes that will make life better. Try to be optimistic and learn to endure hardships without giving up and learn from them. Never forget that the most important thing we can do in our lives as Christians, is to learn all we can about all there is and then give it all away. Find strength in adversity and although your body will someday grow old, keep those beautiful eyes open and your heart forever young.

There will come a day when you begin asking questions. Some of your questions will be difficult to answer. Some of the answers will be difficult for you to hear. Keep those eyes open to the very wonder of why God sent you to us. Keep those eyes open to the people who surround you now and will always be here for you. I have one answer for you before you ever have a chance to ask. Who loves you? More people than you can ever imagine. You are a very special person to so many. God will always keep you as the apple of His eye and protect you, and He has assigned many helpers to watch over you.

PART 3

Season of Questioning

What's Wrong With Common Sense?

*Let those who are wise understand these things. Let those
who are discerning listen carefully. The paths of the
Lord are true and right, and righteous people live by walking
in them. But sinners stumble and fall along the way.*
---Hosea 14:9

    Everyone has a testimony, whether they've accepted Jesus or not. It's the telling that's sometimes hard. It can be shared verbally in just a few words and to an audience of one or read in a 300-page book by millions. God doesn't follow an outline for sharing our personal stories, but He leaves the door wide open for the writer and the reader to search for both truth and understanding of life's unanswered questions.

    At one time I noticed myself going into my bedroom when I was upset or worried. I would sit in my purple chair and open up to any page in the Bible to read. It calmed the anxiety attacks I'd had since leaving California. The feeling of emptiness was quickly being removed. I didn't understand everything that was happening to me but I felt the changes taking place. Soon reading my Bible became part of my daily routine. I placed myself on a Reading through the Bible in One Year schedule. As much as I did not enjoy the Old Testament, I was anxious to read through it a second time to see if I would find answers to my questions. I'm now reading the Old Testament for a third time and a few questions got answered, but many persist.

Liberal or Conservative, which one are you? I can't think of anything more demeaning to one's own intelligence than to hear them categorize people into groups of Liberals and Conservatives. Whatever happened to good sense? A person who can look at all sides without tunnel vision? Someone with street smarts is more meaningful to me than someone throwing out these useless labels. We want our children and grandchildren to be so grounded in their faith and confident in themselves that they can ask questions when they don't understand and listen, really listen, with an open heart and mind when people speak We don't want them to play follow the leader in a group of people because it's easier than standing alone rocking the boat with their own opinions. I speak quite strongly on the subject and have rocked the boat many times.

I've known a man for a few years. I've tried to like him and have asked God to forgive me because I haven't reached that place. This man is so blinded by his conservative label that to call him arrogant won't do justice. I know I have issues with this man and I know God will eventually soften my heart if I don't give up asking for His help. This gentleman insists his translation of scripture is the only right one. Everyone else is doomed for hell.

This gentleman occasionally steps in for the pastor of his church on Sunday mornings. I was told that he spoke this past week on Pleasures of this world. He spoke on the pleasures a wealthy person should enjoy without guilt. I've asked God to control my tongue the few times I've visited that church. I've heard him boast of his riches in front of the less fortunate and downright poor. I've sat restless in my chair as he stood in front of the congregation saying, "God wants me to enjoy my wealth. God wants me to stand on the beautiful Hawaiian beaches, and God says it's OK to have a glass of wine to take the edge off my day."

Most of the congregation in this particular church struggle financially. Most cannot afford vacations of any sort or even pay for medical insurance. Some are recovering alcoholics. God gave more to some than others and I often ask Why? Slowdown and don't work to become rich. Don't store up treasures on this earth, for when we leave these treasures get left behind. A U-Haul is not a common vehicle to be seen in front of a mortuary.

A wonderful thing to believe is that God blesses us when we work hard. We then turn around and share these blessings and watch as more come. I know many people who were born into abundant wealth. There are those who share what they've been given and, if you don't know them, you would not know of their wealth because they don't flaunt it. Then there are those who flaunt in front of the less fortunate, preach how God wants them to enjoy what they have and give only enough to make themselves feel good. Not all the giving is done in secret as God instructed. Maybe from a Biblical point of view these "Look at the good I'm doing" people can be called modern day Pharisees.

No secret to most who know me, there are times I have allowed myself to dream of what I'd do if I were still wealthy. First on the list remains that ready-packed, ready to go, pop-up-tent-trailer, although now I would consider the convenience of a small motor home with an unlimited gasoline card. I have allowed myself to drift off in dreams of traveling across states, loaded with cameras and a laptop, a Bible and my knitting supplies, bicycles and a canoe. Also, skis and snowshoes for winter traveling, a Thermos filled with the finest coffee, and an ample supply of decadent chocolate.

Have you noticed people around you who have so much, but are unhappy? I'm talking about people who have more than the average person can dream of, but turn to unhealthy vices such as alcohol, sex, and drugs? Often it is the result of boredom, depression, and a feeling of emptiness. How many people who have it all commit suicide to escape their misery? We are promised shelter and rest in the shadow of the Almighty. How can someone have it all if they don't have the peace and security that comes from a relationship with Christ?

I've wondered about pastors from different churches in town giving similar sermons on or close to the same Sunday. This morning at a new church, the pastor opened the sermon asking, "Are we supposed to enjoy the pleasures of this world? Yes! God wouldn't have created them if He hadn't meant for them to be enjoyed." But these are pleasures Jesus Christ created to be enjoyed in His name. Pleasures we would not want to hide from Him if He were to come today."

A secret to some is, God is no wimp and He's not a boring guy. He loves to party and He loves to have a good time. Read all about it in His biography. It's been a number one best-selling story for years. You will find it filled with mystery, wonderous surprises, and an endless stream of wisdom, and comfort. Possibly a book you can't put down once you open it and one you may want to read again and again. ***How sweet are Your words to my taste; they are sweeter than honey. Your word is a lamp for my feet and a light for my path. --- Psalms 119:103-105***

My favorite song performed with the kids in our preschool programs was, *What A Wonderful World*. That's what the world would be if everyone believed in the power of prayer. It works! God listens! God answers! I've argued with people who tell me there are certain ways to pray. I can't believe God wants religious robots. They say you cannot get angry with God. I say, hogwash! God wants us to be in constant conversation with Him. He wants us to recognize His blessings and to praise Him. He knows our heart, thoughts and feelings, but He wants us to tell Him anyway.

God doesn't want us to come to Him and pretend everything is hunky-dory when it's not. He wants us to pour out our frustrations, our anger, disappointments, and pain. It is called lamenting to The Almighty whose understanding is beyond our comprehension. It is the only way to having a perfect relationship with our Creator, our Father, our Friend, our Comforter.

A large portion of my complaints come from first-hand experiencing how people with a little power pass on their own outrageous advice, man-made rules, and interpretation of the Bible. You might ask what this has to do with good sense. I have been bothered by the number of people who agree with what these self-righteous leaders say in everything from who can sing in the church choir, when the Bible says to make a joyful sound unto the Lord, to how we are to pray.

I heard the most absurd sermon ever delivered last year on a popular Christian radio station. The pastor was explaining the proper way to pray. His way was formal, cold and choreographed. He told parents how wrong it is to teach a child to recite prayers. He used *Now I Lay Me Down to Sleep* as an example. Not only did he recite the prayer, but he also added a horrible, whiny voice in his presentation. If I hadn't been so angry, I would have laughed. I believe we are to teach our little ones to recite these children's prayers in the very beginning of their lives. In my opinion, these little prayers will grow into bigger prayers coming straight from our children's hearts.

I know how busy you are, so when do you find time to pray?" My friend Kirsten asked. I'm busy. Often busier than I would like to be when I pray? I like to slip out of the bed and slide into my purple chair waiting only inches away. If I know it's going to be one of those days when the wheels on my invisible roller skates, as my friend Cricket puts it, don't stop, I pray before crawling out from under the bedding. When I know I'm not going to be rushed, I love sitting in my backyard watching little critters scamper throughout my garden, and with the warmth of morning sunshine on my face, pray with my eyes wide open.

I fall into the same routine as many of you. At night I wait until I crawl into bed and, you probably guessed it, the following morning I wake up realizing I never made it to the Amen. I speak with God all day long, anytime, anyplace, and He listens. The first time I realized this, I was standing under a hot shower shampooing my hair. "God I can't stop talking to You. I can't turn me off" I said. What's wrong with me?" then I read in the Bible I was doing the most important thing God wants us to do. I was communicating with Him continuously. What an awesome thing to share with our children. We are never alone.

Although I have grown in my faith and I no longer need to write prayers to drop in my prayer box, I have people who call and ask me to drop prayers in for them. I don't know everything tomorrow holds and what little I might know, I don't always understand. I'm coming closer each day to not worrying about the future because I know who holds my hand.

I know for sure God doesn't care how we pray as long as we just do it. He listens and if we do the same, we will learn to know His voice when He speaks. *I love the Lord because He hears and answers my prayers. Because He bends down and listens, I will pray as long as I have breath! --Psalms 116:1-2*

Is God An Unloving God?

Be self-controlled and alert. Your enemy the devil prowls around like a roaring lion looking for someone to devour. Resist him, standing firm in your faith, because you know that your brothers throughout the world are undergoing the same kind of sufferings.
---1 Peter 5:8-9

I've heard Satan described as someone who comes in sheep's clothing. I've heard Satan described as someone who, if he doesn't win you over with his cunning ways, discards his disguise and pounds on your door and rattles the windows. Satan will do anything to get your attention. The stronger our faith, the harder Satan has to work. There has been speculation on recent natural disasters: Satan delights in painting God as unloving.

I am not a Bible scholar and while my mind is filled with coherent thoughts, putting them on paper is not easy. Maybe the best description for what I'm trying to convey is through a news clip I saw of a resident on the island where the devastating tsunami struck in Thailand. The tormented woman was tossing worship idols from her home. Her family was dead and realizing their worthlessness, she screamed at the idols that sat doing nothing. *Their idols are merely things of silver and gold, shaped by human hands. They cannot talk, though they have mouths, or see, though they have eyes! They cannot hear with their ears, or smell with their noses, or feel with their hands, or walk with their feet, or utter sounds with their throats! And those who make them are just like them, as are all who trust in them.* "---Psalms 115:4-8

Tragedies happen every day, big and small, private or making headlines around the world. Some people are sinking under the high cost of living, the majority of us are treading water, and those sitting on mountain tops want more. These are man-made problems. Yes, God may allow humans to mess up the planet and allow natural disasters which some call Acts of God. I don't believe He is looking down and targeting bad people. I do believe He uses these tragedies to bring attention to Himself, giving a picture of what is to come and what is possible to avoid. A question comes to me as I type. I've already admitted I have a problem with bedside salvation. Yet, if bedside salvation is real, isn't it possible to be saved as strong hurricane winds kill you or rushing tides pull you under? Will these newly saved souls be remembered as bad people?

Fear is a common issue in these present times and one of which I have so little understanding. The Bible teaches us to trust in God, do not worry, do not be afraid, for He is with us and will protect us always. So many verses throughout the Bible relay the same message. Why then are so many Christians afraid of what is happening around them, which is actually what the Book tells us will take place? Why did President Bush, the man elected to the highest position in our government put into action a color code to warn the America people daily of the level of fear to have? While advertising his Christian faith and belief in the Bible, does this man have doubts in God's promises? I know we are human, but if we are grounded in our faith, as we say we are, then where does fear come from?

There was an older couple who had been members of a church here in Tumalo since the doors first opened. The gentleman was as knowledgeable of the Good Book as a pastor should be. He researched and then moved his wife thousands of miles from Bend to live where he said was "the safest place to be when the Y2K strikes." Our Christian growth and trust in God's protection doesn't happen overnight. I guess for some it takes a lifetime of searching and some never find it.

Why do bad things happen to good people? This remains one of God's greatest unanswered questions and probably will until we stand before Him. We need to remember that God is in control. There will come a day when God does pour His wrath on evil people, but I don't believe it's happening now as some claim. Our God works around the clock showing us His power and offering His forgiveness. God wants no one left behind and the Bible tells us that most of us will come to Him through our worst pain. Some of the best instructions we can pass on to our children is the knowledge we have of a loving God and that we don't have to understand how He works. If we did, He would be just like us.

Yesterday afternoon I did something I seldom do. Kirsten and her mother came for lunch and when they left, I turned on the television to watch the latest news on Hurricane Katrina. Again, I felt humbled. It set off dozens of questions. This is America, the land of milk and honey? The country whose people come first? I felt ashamed. What is so important about me that others will want to read my story? I thought I had an answer, but yesterday's news brought doubts.

My brain doesn't want to shut down. I keep wondering how God will answer my question. I'm hoping to make a statement for Christ, but do I really know how to do this? I don't want someone to read my story and be turned off from knowing God because of something I've said. These hurricane victims are suffering much more than I ever did. While the media turns cameras to the South, focus on our young Americans and innocent people in Iraq fade into the backdrop. Why would a loving God permit the horror and pain being afflicted around the world?

I caught another glimpse of news. One segment was on a popular Madame whose book names some of her most famous Hollywood clients. Another book being published by a Hollywood celebrity is a children's book on the Kabbalah religion and is now said to have been written by a ghost writer. I'm not known outside my little circle of family and friends, but the main character of my story is. What chance do I have in competing with these writers?

Ever feel you are sitting between hearing God tell you the plans He has for you and your own imagination showing you what you want? We know God wants to give us His best, yet have you ever wondered while waiting for answers to prayer, just how painful it might turn out to be if there is a lesson to be learned?

I sat last night listening to a talk show coming from the other room. I immediately turned it off when a comedian using foul language began mocking Christianity and portrayed Jesus as the goofy guy. I wondered if the comedian is pleased with his act when he goes home and there is no audience. I'm stretching my imagination when I think maybe I can help open someone's eyes to the choice they have of a world of empty promises or a God of true fulfillment.

It's Just Stuff

Stuff: raw material ready to go into some manufacturing process; personal property; rubbish; trash; to crowd in; to feel greedily.
---Webster's Dictionary

Many of us have heard the saying, "We are tallest when we are down on our knees." The gracious invitation that God extends to us is to come to Him anytime, anywhere, and just as we are. No Hollywood makeover and no pretending we're someone we're not. I opened a fortune cookie recently that read, "Faith is your answer to success." God, the author of creativity, stands with open arms as He teaches us through temporary earthy trials, that we can have it all if we only believe in Him.

Believing in Jesus and setting out on our Christian walk is no tiptoeing through the tulips. It's a difficult hike to reach that steep mountaintop. We may get scraped by craggy rocks. Blisters may form on our feet. There may come a time when we want to give up. But going ahead through life without God can be lonely and carry a very high price with it. There is a vacant chair at the Lord's dining table waiting just for you. Don't make excuses. RSVP now.

I do think people can best share a message of hope with someone if they have suffered in similar situations and pain. There have been many times I've asked God to choose another family to share this hope, but God has His own agenda. I remind myself that nothing can touch us that God hasn't permitted, always with our best interest at heart. He shares in the bad times as well as the good. "Dear God, I know you will provide, but why don't you provide until you provide?" I've been told is an old Jewish proverb. I didn't understand it at first, but after reading it several times, it began making sense, at least I think it did. We must remember we are in training for whatever God has planned, and since

He is our personal body trainer and the church is our gym, the best we can do is follow without complaints.

The eyes of the Lord range throughout the universe. I believe this. I'm comforted knowing God is watching over me and my loved ones. When I receive the "Everything is wonderful at our house" Christmas letters and messages throughout the year from friends and acquaintances, I often battle with my emotions. We are told to live by faith, not by our emotions. Not easy to do when you're drowning in trials and feel you are the only one they missed when life jackets were handed out. Before accepting Christ and growing stronger in my faith, these "Everything is wonderful at our house" letters left me days in depression and I was angry and envious of their happy lives. I hopelessly wondered, and occasionally still do, why these people seem to never have anything taken from them and seem to have the best of everything. Why do some of us make sacrifices and others seem to sail on smooth waters their entire lives? It's another of God's unanswered questions.

Do they think I'm nuts for eliminating the skeletons in my closet which controlled my life until sharing them? Do they understand the freedom I've gained from this? How many of these perfect lives are actually hiding their own skeletons?

How will these people who have lived an abundant life, react if some morning they wake up and find it gone as we did? Will they run and try to hide from their problems as I did? Will they have already learned the power of perseverance through Christ, which unfortunately took me precious time to uncover? Scripture tells us that the wealthy and those who have everything will eventually go through the greatest testing.

Will these good people if asked, with all these worldly privileges at their fingertips, give it away to follow Christ? *As Jesus started on His way, a man ran up to Him and fell on his knees before Him. "Good Teacher," he said, "what must I do to inherit eternal life?" Jesus looked at him and loved him. "One thing you lack," He said. "Go sell everything you have and give it to the poor, and you will have treasure in heaven. Then come, follow Me." At this the man's face fell. He went away sad because he had great wealth. Jesus looked around and said to His disciples, "How hard it is for the rich to enter the kingdom of God!" ---Mark 10:17. 21-23*

The Walking Shoes

These questions at times have played in my head like a recording set on repeat. Wisdom comes through experiences and often not without pain. I believe, but don't fully understand, that we are where God wants us to be. If I understood this I might understand why I thank God for allowing my family to toss out the rose-colored glasses and see, and experience the struggles in this world, and because we lack the stuff we thought would fill the void in our lives, feel true compassion for others. Taking away the stuff in our lives was part of God's plan. He has better things to occupy our lives. God is the One controlling our destiny and what He has waiting for us in heaven is not just stuff.

PART 4

Season of Frustration

God's Pause Button

**Be still and know that I am God!
—Psalms 46: 10**

    I closed my bedroom door this morning and let out a quiet sigh as I pushed the invisible pause button God provides. Feeling my body sink into the comfortable purple chair sitting next to the bed, I closed my eyes. The world was hectic outside those four walls, and right at that moment I needed to remove myself from it and talk with Jesus. I'm surrounded by loved ones, but not one can bring the peace that God does and certainly not as quickly, when these earthly walls begin closing in on me.

    Do you believe in the old tale about finding a money tree to solve a person's problems and they live happily-ever-after? I've read too many stories about lottery winners and Hollywood celebrities to believe in such a thing. We have watched as instant millionaires who have lived empty, lonely lives, believing money could resolve their problems, become emptier, lonelier, and broke. We have watched as countless celebrities desire more than the amount of money and fame already gained and continue living unsatisfied lives. The popular religion among celebrities today is training them not to accept belief or faith. To me this spells E-M-P-T-I-N-E-S-S.

There are TV commercials displaying an "easy button" to get us out of difficult situations. What I'm looking for is my personal pause button. A button always at my fingertips to push when life gets too rushed, too scary, or just too complicated. When my eyes seem to cross and my hair stands straight up like a troll doll. Oh, to have such a button in my possession.

I remember when I would have given up caffeine, coffee and chocolate for the rest of my life to have this unique button. My husband had an appointment that afternoon with his heart specialist. Our son in California had been released from the hospital that morning after contracting food poisoning from a popular Sacramento restaurant. Our son living in Bend was suffering from gray Central Oregon weather and missing California sunshine and beaches. Our daughter was uncomfortable and irritable nearing the delivery of her baby. All I wished for was to see everyone happy, including myself.

This morning as I went into my room and closed the door, I had an overwhelming urge to have a pity party. Instead, I did what I know is the right thing to do in times like these. It took years to discover that nothing heals quicker than prayer and focusing on the good things we have seen God work in our lives. Often through the worst of times we can see God reveal life changing truth. So, I prayed. I began as I always do by asking God to forgive my sins and those of my loved ones. I searched deeper into this all- too-familiar request. The parable about God sowing good seeds amongst the weeds and my own conclusion that the closer we come to Christ, the fewer weeds seem to come into my garden crowded my thinking.

I carry with me a mental list of loved ones I pray for each day and asking God to forgive their sins has sadly become routine. But what sins am I or my loved ones actually burdened with? I scrolled down the list of special people searching for an answer. Unlike many friends in my past, I found no great sin. At this point I was reminded again of my garden and how few weeds have grown in it since I began my walk with

Christ. It seems most on my list have accepted Christ as their personal Savior and those who haven't are so very near.

I was reminded that we all sin and no matter the sin, a sin is a sin in God's eyes. I've changed the way I pray. Aware that sin starts in the mind, I ask that our minds be filled with pure thoughts and our hearts transformed into a heart like Jesus. I ask to learn to love others like Jesus does. I also ask for more people to come into my garden.

"Thank you Jesus for our blessings" I said. Funny, saying thank you this morning wasn't enough. I closed my eyes again and remembering the wonderful things God has provided, I asked that He hear our praises for who He is and for loving us as He does. My mind wandered from one blessing to the next. I was given such a clear vision of how many of these blessings came after witnessing myself and my loved ones persevering through some of our biggest sorrows. Tears filled my eyes as I praised Jesus for keeping a firm grip on our hand as He walked beside us, as we climbed to a mountain top only to fall back down in the valley. God was there with us during these trials, making it hard for us to sit down and refuse to go on. If ever in doubt of the power of God or the way He mysteriously works in our lives, be still and do as I do. Sit back and be glad that the Almighty is sitting in the pilot's seat. *No eye has seen, no ear has heard, no mind has conceived what God has prepared for those who love Him. ---1 Corinthians 2:9*

Innocence of a Child

They are like trees planted along a riverbank, with roots that reach deep into the water. Such trees are not bothered by the heat or worried by long months of drought. Their leaves stay green, and they go right on producing delicious fruit.
---Jeremiah 17:8

Wouldn't it be wonderful if only for a little while, to slip back into those days when we were innocent children? When we could play in the heat of the summer or the cold of winter and keep a smile on our face, without complaining about the weather? Trusting everyone. Unaware that people can have alternative motives for gaining our trust. It is no mystery to me, why God wants us to become a child in our acceptance of faith. He tells us, "Only the children will enter heaven," I can't imagine a child standing at the gates of heaven, asking, "Shall I enter?"

We don't have to understand God's ways, just trust in Him like a child whose eyes are filled with wonder. An exasperated mother, whose son was always getting into mischief, finally asked him *"How do you expect to get into heaven?" The boy thought it over and said, "Well, I'll run in and out and in and out and keep slamming doors until St. Peter says, "For heaven's sake, Dylan, come in or stay out!" ---Anonymous*

We were eating dinner in a downtown restaurant last night, when I shared with my husband some thoughts I had concerning yesterday's sermon. And the Polish sausage from Costco. One day I had picked up sausages for lunch for me and my son. I usually talk myself out of buying them and smothering them in sauerkraut, mustard, onions and relish. But on that particular day, I couldn't resist. With the aroma of sausages filling my car, tempting me to pull back the foil and munch on my way home, I passed the Rite-Aid drug store. What I saw made me stop and turn in. A lonely, grubby-looking man was standing with a sign asking for food.

I walked into the drug store and picked up some chips and a box of chocolates. I rolled my window down and handed him the bag, my sausage and a soda. I'm aware that not all beggars are honest people. Some make a good living from panhandling. Many years ago in California, a newspaper investigated the problem and its article was amazing. Some of these beggars owned beautiful homes, nice vehicles, and had bank accounts. This man seemed grateful, giving me a good feeling to carry with me the rest of the week.

The following week on our drive to Costco, we passed the drug store. A young man stood in the same spot. "I know what you want to do," my husband said, and he was right. We packed up a hot lunch and drove back to the parking lot to where the young man was standing. I was taken aback when we offered the food and he quickly replied, "No thanks, I'd rather have money."

What I got from Sunday's sermon and the sausage events, confirms the idea that what we are sure we see, can turn out to be something very different. Life is more complicated than picking off daisy petals and saying, "He loves me, he loves me not," and leaving life to chance. What some people hear coming from the Bible may be the emotions of a flippant person, a person who sees God the way he wants God to be. Something that should not be taken lightly.

Lord of All

For there is no difference between Jew and Gentile---the same Lord is Lord of all and richly blesses all who call on Him, "Everyone who calls on Him will be saved."
---Romans 10:12-13

Being a Christian means we should be open to listening to what someone else has to say about their faith and be ready to share ours. Pastor told us in his sermon. "Sometimes this might be a conversation between Christians." Three years ago, my husband was attending church with me, when we experienced just the opposite take place. My husband walked in, shook hands with the pastor and commented on the headlines of the morning newspaper. The pastor told him, "Your opinions are wrong!"

What happened next I would compare to an emergency crew rushing to the scene of a disaster. The pastor, waving his hands like a traffic cop, called church elders over and instructed them to convince my husband to change his views on the matter. What had gotten the pastor so panic stricken was David agreeing with the article claiming there are other religions who worship the same God as we do, just in different ways. Another day while shopping in Costco, a prominent church member walked up and told my husband, "If you don't believe in Jesus Christ you are going to hell." This same man left the church in a huff the following week when he was asked to tone down his beautiful but loud, singing voice during choir rehearsal.

Verse 3:15 in the Book of Peter instructs Christians to share their hope in Jesus with gentleness and respect. I'd say these people must have skipped over the verse. These self-righteous people turned my husband in the opposite direction Jesus wanted him to go. Pastor at our new church says, "It's not up to you to change people. Your responsibility is to show love and let God handle the rest." Reaching out to someone who is different than we are is a beautiful example of unconditional love.

How easy is it to make mistakes when we listen and too often accept another's opinions without evaluating our own? We are told as Christians we must believe the Bible to be true. We are told we must follow the Bible's instructions from cover to cover. This comes directly off the pages of the Bible. No other book has stayed on the best seller's list as long, which makes a huge statement when someone tries to challenge it.

The problem I do have, or people have with me, is my inability to follow the thoughts and instructions of someone who sees scripture totally different than I do. What are the right words to say to someone who in my opinion, has forgotten that God hates sin, yet hasn't met a sinner He doesn't love. The only thing that can separate us from God is not believing He sent His Son to die for our sins.

We need church leaders, but not those who are closed minded, who do all the talking and never listen. God gave the Bible to use as a resource of comfort and energy. He shows Himself as a vine and invites us to be the branches growing from it. As long as we are part of that vine, God will open our minds to think clearly and it is our responsibility to search the Bible for the spiritual knowledge needed to understand His ways. We don't have to wear ourselves out trying to be the perfect Christian. The Lord is the only one who is perfect.

Looking For La-la

And you must love your neighbor just as much as you love yourself...
---Luke 10:27 TLB

"Oh, let the sunshine in," the kids' voices sang out during each of our programs. Take a moment and ponder the words to that song. "Mommy told me something that a little kid should know, it's all about the devil and I've learned to hate him so." The song speaks of how the devil wears a grin when we wear a frown. It also speaks of the devil jumping for joy when we forget to pray. But when the devil sees us wearing a smile or down on our knees talking to Jesus, he knows he has lost all power over us.

I sit imagining the sound of my own children's voices echoing "la-la" when I'm no longer with them. According to them, this made-up word means wholesome, sweet and clean. It applies to the type of movies, music, books, people, and just about everything I enjoy. It wouldn't surprise me if they had used words such as prude, prissy, boring, to describe their mother when they were teenagers. Can you imagine living in a world where everyone finds hating the devil and loving Jesus simple? Can you imagine every mother reciting these basic instructions at birth and children never finding it necessary to ask why?

I see life on earth as one fantastic voyage and we never know when it will end. As soon as Christ enters into our hearts, He sails right along with us. No matter the size of pitfalls we may find ourselves facing, our Lord will protect and reassure us as we travel His pathway. This topsy-turvy life is temporary and the glory of heaven awaits us. My purpose of writing is not to self-righteously judge and condemn those who aren't believers. It's not my job or calling, and I in no way want such a responsibility. But the restlessness inside wants to tell these people to seek truth, which may differ for every individual under the sun. To not just fit into the crowd, a sheep following the wrong shepherd. There are many good shepherds, but sorry to say in today's society there is also a large number of bad ones.

Think of opening the morning newspaper or turning on the morning news channel and finding good things happening to start your day. When my husband begins to read out loud from the morning paper, I challenge him to find something happy to share. As he read the article written in *The Sunday Oregonian*, July 23, 2006, we both cried. The story introduced us to a young man who has been walking in Job's shoes. In the past year, this man has lost his wife to a rare blood disease, lost his job in the slow economy and lost his home. He is raising three well-adjusted kids who know their father's love and have learned to smile along with him. This young man is a sad man, but he isn't a bitter man. True compassion is given to us from God as a gift to give away. I believe He challenges us on a daily basis to use it to meet the needs of others. One week later, readers of *The Sunday Oregonian* rallied together pouring out their love and support to this family. People offered employment, a place to live, and financial help. What a wonderful example of that la-la world I'm looking for.

There are ways we as Christians can reach out and help those in need and at the same time show God's love. The list of opportunities to help is longer than any list of Christian gripes pertaining to lifestyles, protecting criminals, and whose interpretation of scripture ranks the highest on the charts, to name a few.

Be a conspicuous Christian. Don't embellish by adding liberal, conservative, evangelical, or any of the other titles in today's vocabulary. Reach out with good deeds and the light of your faith will shine on others. The response from readers of the *Oregonian*, for the young father and his children is a heartwarming example of understanding what having a heart that mirrors Jesus' is all about.

He Knows Our Thoughts

But, I desire to speak to the Almighty and to argue my case before God. Though He slay me, yet I will have hope in Him; I will surely defend my ways to His face. Indeed, this will turn out for my deliverance, for no godless man would dare come before Him.
---Job 13:3, 15-16

I find myself questioning people and digging deeper into the Bible far more than I ever have. I want to understand, not judge, those who say they live by the Bible yet insist on picking and choosing what is good or bad, which coincidently fits their lifestyles. Since I don't live in a la-la world, I have found endless passages to help explain why I believe Christians can ask questions regarding scripture, and at times argue their cases before God and before their peers. No matter what you're feeling, God wants to hear from you.

I don't believe God wants us to be religious robots and let our faith become humdrum. Groups may spend their time and energy, which could be put to better use, in arguing the **Darwin Theory**, the making of **"The Passion of The Christ"** or the **"Da Vinci Code."** I see that as a battle of the minds, asking questions about Jesus. Why get involved in such an uproar? Why get yourself in a tizzy? What an opportunity to keep our hearts on fire and our souls ignited. What better way to feed our appetites for learning, than to study His word and be able to share, although it may resemble a debate, with non- believers? People around us may disguise their desires to know more about our faith. Instead of taking a leap in faith, too many of us sometimes choose to protect our own self-image and remain silent.

I'm starting through the Bible a fourth time and I never know what buried treasure I will find. Each time I read through His word, I find that God is uncovering more secrets and handing out more blessings, allowing my family greater understanding of the continuous tough times with which we are bombarded. I can read the same passages time and time again and suddenly see them shine on the pages like a neon sign flashing new meaning.

Living together before marriage is possibly the rule broken most often. I have a friend who has been married to the same man for half a century. It's not that she doesn't love him or didn't know this man before marrying but being young she believed they were two hearts with a dream for sharing the future together. Not only in everyday chores and sickness but enjoying fun times and making memories as a couple and as a family.

"We have to start doing things together," she confronted her husband twenty-five years ago. "We don't have to do things together to have a good marriage," was his reply. So, for the next twenty-five years, while sharing no common interest and having little to talk about when they do talk, she has watched life pass her by. Could this have been avoided by the couple trying marriage on to make sure it was the right fit? I don't appreciate the phrase, but most people understand it.

There is scripture claiming women cannot become pastors and women are to submit totally to their husbands. I once befriended a woman who submitted to her husband. She never questioned him on biblical issues or any other issue of which I'm aware. I had admired the way the couple were raising their small children. The kids had no squabble over being home schooled. They were well manned, obedient and not once did I hear an argumentative word spoken to the parents. Then the girls grew into young women and I slowly discovered the lifestyle of this family was not what I would choose. I slowly discovered their lifestyle was not one I would choose for my daughter or my granddaughter. They were so overly protected that it became apparent they had been cut off from the reality of living of the outside world.

There are those who consider themselves loving parents and good teachers of the Bible. Rightly so, as long as their children obey biblical doctrine as they see it. A person can be led down a difficult path of unnecessary obstacles to overcome while on their Christian walk, if they are led into listening to wrong thinking. The only failsafe protection is to have a clear understanding of scripture.

I witnessed this happening to the family to which I had at one time felt close to. Dating is not permitted. During courtship the women are not allowed to talk to men in person, or e-mail with a man or have a conversation with a man on the telephone, unless approved and supervised by her parents. Interested men must realize they are not courting the girl, but her entire family. He must state his intentions for the future and realize he marries not only the girl, but her entire family. They must abide by her father's rules after marriage.

The parents put aside the rule concerning e-mailing and a twenty-one-year-old daughter was given permission to e-mail with a young gentleman. All incoming and outgoing e-mail was first read and approved by the girl's father. After several months of e-mailing with the Christian man who had a college education and a good job, money in the bank to buy a home and a desire to marry and raise a family, the relationship was brought to an abrupt end by her father.

The daughter had begun to make plans for the future, unknown to the young man, and the pen-pal was asked by her father, by e-mail, what his intentions were for marriage. Dumb founded, the young man offered his best possible answer. "I don't know," he said. "I'm interested in your daughter. I want to meet her and this is a question to be answered when we meet, and speak, and when we know each other." He was told by the girl's father not to contact his daughter again.

The best spiritual covering we can have is to know when Satan knocks and we ask Jesus to open the door, He won't hesitate. "The Bible clearly states the duties of the husband," the girl's father replied. The human emotional side wants to continue this discussion. I want to let this man know I see him as a blooming idiot and that he needs to sweep his own door mat before attempting to sweep someone else's. If we teach our children the right way to live, we have done what God has asked us to do. We then give to our children the gift of trust. If we don't do this or allow our children to grow into self-sufficient adults, we have failed at the job God gave us. I know the best thing to do for this man is to pray for him.

A Mystery and No Clues

Whatever wisdom may be, it is far off and most profound--who can discover it? So, I turned my mind to understand to investigate and to search out wisdom and the scheme of things and to understand the stupidity of wickedness and the madness of folly.
--Ecclesiastes 7:24-25

The clouds have disappeared and as the sky darkens, the first star of the evening is shining brightly. Knowing we don't live in a la-la world, my mind turns from the innocence of the cloud game to the questions that have been troubling me for some time now. Homosexuality and capital punishment have been two of the hottest topics around for decades in this problematic world. These subject matters have provided an overwhelming supply of material for the media to play with, while attempts to degrade Christianity never stop. It makes me wonder how reporters, TV hosts and comedians would behave in heaven where there is no one to gossip about or poke fun at, a place where everyone really does love their neighbor.

It puzzles me how some Christians, while strongly agreeing with the Bible on homosexuality, disregard what the Bible says about a person committing murder. Although I believe the Bible to be true, I also believe God has a purpose for some people being born with a need for a lifestyle that differs from that of others, a lifestyle that in most cases is shunned without concern for what made that person who he or she is.

God speaks throughout the Bible on the importance of loving each other. Man cannot know everything the Lord has planned for us. We cannot see ahead to the testing we will go through in our lifetime. What if the most important test is how we love each other? How many of you can say you have loved people who live different lifestyles and you have placed no obstacles between them and Jesus? Have you never been guilty of turning your back on one of these people before knowing them? Have you never shunned another person, forgetting what Jesus said about cleaning up your own act before tossing that first stone?

Any church leader, in my mind, who uses the words "disgusting" and "detestable" when speaking on homosexuality, instead of telling the congregation that they should act as one thirsty person leading another to water, is contradicting scripture. No matter our title or position, each of us needs to take time out regularly to take inventory of our spiritual lives. Do we have in our hearts what a true Christian has? Do we do wise things such as read our Bibles every day, pray continuously, and go to church? More importantly, are we living our faith on a fulltime schedule or are we a one-hour-a-week Christian? Are we growing or are we backsliding?

If we place stumbling blocks, instead of empathy, between another person and Christ, that is a sin. "Sin can make us stupid," is a statement I don't want to forget. **With the tongue we praise our Lord and Father, and with it we curse men, who have been made in God's likeness. Out of the mouth come praise and cursing. My brothers, this should not be. ---James 3:9-10**

I recently overheard a young mom saying that her son was in Cub Scouts and how it is strongly Christian based. "No gays are allowed to be leaders," was the next thing out of her mouth. I walked away a bit confused. How does one portray herself as a Christian while disobeying God's commandment to love everyone and not judge.

The Walking Shoes

I'm not angry, but I do get frustrated seeing the actions of those who throw stones. In my heart I believe God has a reason for some to have a different lifestyle, perhaps resulting from something horrendous happening to them at a young age or pain and suffering as a child they had no control over. Instead of all Christians treating this as such or considering what purpose God may have for allowing this to happen, many are controlled by a judgmental spirit. **God works everything for the good of those who love Him.**

A former professional football star discovered a world of rejection after announcing to the world that he was gay. As a young boy, his mother sent him to someone's house to help with cleaning chores. The wife left, leaving the boy alone in the house with her husband, who raped him. This young man spent years living with secrets. He spent years confused, unhappy, and wondering who he was. When this football star made the announcement being gay on a TV show, the life he knew to be difficult became a nightmare. Today this same person finds himself, after finding Christ, at peace and knowing who he is. He is a messenger of God and shares his past as a way to help others who carry scars from childhood.

The Bible clearly states that homosexuality is wrong. But what is right about people who call themselves Christians who murder a homosexual, or a physician and his staff who perform legal abortions, or anyone else for that matter, using the excuse of doing it in the name of God? As a Christian burdened with feelings to condemn another human being, have you ever taken time to ask, "If you had a choice would you have chosen this life for yourself?" How many people do you think would answer yes and turn down what is considered normal, in exchange for the struggles and hardships involved in this already difficult world in which we live? There are times when my mind searches for a "default" button to change the lives that differ from mine and lessen their burdens.

Would I be concerned about the treatment of gays if God had not placed them in my life? I don't know. God always seems to bring good out of situations and I want to remember this if I start to doubt myself. With these people in my life, I can't avoid knowing who they are and why they are who they are. The Bible says God has a purpose for everything under the sun. I take this literally. God wants us to share love, not condemnation until His return.

It is easy for someone to neglect what the Bible says about God making us all in His image. God would rather go to hell for you than go to heaven without you, is a most powerful line. God hates sin, but we are all God's children and His banner of love covers everyone. He promises to love us as we are, but He will do His best to move us into the place He wants us to be, often using another person to do this. He wants everyone to spend eternity with Him. At least that's what I hear coming from the Bible. Otherwise, when we sing "Jesus loves me, this I know, for the Bible tells me so," is it a lie? I trust God with my life, but I know He doesn't mind when I lock my doors, take my meds, and carry a spare tire in my car. One of the first things we should teach our children or our grandchildren, is to believe God will keep them safe, but also to hold our hand, know when to say "No!" and how to dial 911. I don't believe God has a problem accepting my doubts as He watches me becoming firmly rooted in His word and truth. He knows my doubts come from a personal journey of searching, in order to have a closer walk with Him.

"Faith is the focus of the Bible. It is the story of how Jesus came to jump start man's faith in God, not a group of people discussing how to reach God" my young son said. Rules and regulations have taken center stage over our personal worship time. One of the most important things to remember when we begin studying Christianity, is that the do's and don'ts of a church have nothing whatsoever to do with our relationship with Christ.

God gave us the Commandments as a guide to living a godly life. "If we have no problems with the first five, we will not have a problem with the next five. The problem in our country is that too many people have a problem with the first five commandments," pastor said on a Christian radio station. The first five have to do with respecting God and the second five are about living our daily lives with other people. I've often been discouraged by those in charge of enforcing the rules and regulations in church. Distracted, I've found myself taking my eyes off the most important thing I'm to do, which is to worship Jesus.

Believers are to be strengthened by other believers. Christians are to be lights for nonbelievers. It is obvious Satan uses discouragement as a tool when believers disagree. Picking and choosing from the Bible what might win votes, while refusing to admit doubt or blame casts a shadow where a bright light is needed. ***God is light; in Him there is no darkness at all. If we claim to have fellowship with Him yet walk in the darkness, we lie and do not live by truth. But if we walk in the light, as He is in the light, we have fellowship with one another, and the blood of Jesus, His Son, purifies us from all sin• ... John 1:5-7***

Being a child of God, in my mind, is to read the Bible and pray, and know that God doesn't expect us to have all the answers. What God wants from us is to never stop searching for a greater understanding of the Bible. He wants us to use our personal experiences in life to see how He works for the good of those who love Him. God wants us to ask Him for guidance and for us to stop judging others. Above all else, God wants us to love one another as He loves us. I've been told to understand God's word we must keep adding fuel. I hope my writing can serve as a type of this valuable fuel.

EPILOGUE

The following recipe is dedicated to all the beautiful Ladies in Pink. A special thank you goes to Dr. Erin Walling my surgeon, Dr. Heather West my medical oncologist, and Dr. Linyee Chang my radiation oncologist along with the other amazing caregivers at St. Charles Hospital, St Charles Cancer Center and Bend Memorial Clinic.

RECIPE FOR SMILES

My friend Erin would soon be arriving with her son for their piano lesson. I brewed a pot of coffee, thinking the robust taste of fine dark roast beans and the coffee aroma coming from upstairs in the kitchen might ease her pain from sitting under my control down in the music room. I made the coffee and poured myself a cup, and funny, it lacks in both fragrance and color, and the taste is far from being robust. Erin agrees it's a little weak, but it's OK. I later e-mail Erin with my special recipe: "Add one pot of sparkling water and forget to dump the morning's coffee grounds."

I received a thank you note from Chris, a friend in California, for two recipes I sent to her Harvard-bound daughter, Kathryn. Kathryn is fortunate to have taken cooking lessons with her father at some wonderful restaurants. My first recipe was for poached eggs. Using a new gadget for the microwave, a few experimental tries and I have the dang thing down, or I think I do. Only three seconds to go and the dang thing explodes. I grab my cameras and a chair and snap some remarkable shots of these luminous yellow and white objects stuck to the far back wall and clinging from the roof of the microwave. My husband shakes his head when he walks in and finds me standing on the chair with my head inside the microwave and says, "The day you do something simple is the day I worry."

I first heard these words when he came home from work to find his new bride had laid six bunches of fresh spinach leaves to dry on top of paper towels spread over kitchen countertops and the living room furniture. After all, the recipe did say to wash and dry thoroughly before making the salad.

My second recipe calls for more ingredients, time and patience. One night I make a pizza, from scratch of course, and it isn't your ordinary run-of-the-mill pizza. This pizza is the most perfect I have ever made, and I grab my camera to take a photo before popping the pie into the oven. There is some shredded mozzarella in the freezer so I pull the pizza out quickly and toss the cheese on top. The feel of the cheese is a bit icy, but it will melt. Timer goes off and the cheese hasn't melted so I pop it back in for the same length of time. Timer goes off again and, instead of a melting ooze of red sauce and white cheese with flavors ready to please, there is absolutely no change. Well, after a trip to the oven and eighty minutes of baking, I notice that the tips of the shredded cheese are beginning to toast and think to myself, "Can it be?" Slowly opening the freezer door, I spy the package of frozen mozzarella cheese. I had put frozen hash brown potatoes on my glorious pizza.

You might think after all these years I'd be done with kitchen mishaps, but no. This evening, I cleaned up after dinner and then went into the bedroom to recheck the to-do list I'd compiled to make getting up and on the road quicker tomorrow morning.

Returning to the kitchen I poured a glass of wine for later in case I have trouble falling asleep. The last thing on my list was to set up the morning coffee. I filled the grinder with special beans my young friends Jenna and Kirsten Maureen had given me for Christmas. Placing the lid on top I pushed down and nothing happened. Removing the top, I could see a small speck of previously grinded coffee had clogged the connection point. "This is an easy fix," I said confidently. With butter knife in hand, I had barely touched the button when the explosion sent beans flying every which way.

A ghastly scream and a hysterical outburst of laughter, which must have sounded like screeches from someone in excruciating pain, brought my husband running to my rescue. The black coffee beans resembling large mouse droppings lay inside, around, behind, on top of and under everything. The only object left untouched was the elegant crystal goblet holding my wine.

The horrified look on his face didn't help to calm the laughter. On cue my husband stood shaking his head saying, "The day you do something simply is the day I worry." And as usual he didn't offer to

The Walking Shoes

help clean up my mess. With the kitchen once again clean, I walked to the bedroom sipping the wine sooner than anticipated.

In the morning, I close my eyes and take a moment for a few deep breaths on the ride into town. My mind recaptures the sound of our laughter, and the beauty and depth of the love we have shared for over fifty-two years. I see the smiles on my son, Michael and his new bride's faces during an enchanted holiday wedding. I almost chuckle out loud remembering Eric and Michael's usual bear-hugs on Christmas Eve, clueless about me being diagnosed with breast cancer a month earlier and sore from the biopsy the day before. The beautiful dark eyes of my daughter, Annette, and the dimples on my granddaughter Alexandra's smiling face appear before me, reminding me of God's miracles.

When the kids returned home from their Honeymoon, it was time to share my secret. They then shared with me my granddaughter, Kayla, was on her way.

Life often deals us wild cards we'd rather place back into the deck. But we must never lock God out of our lives. No matter how ugly the world gets we need to engrain in our hearts that God will protect us. He will turn each painful situation into a blessing if we only allow Him to do so. We may never know why God allows difficulties to come our way.

I sometimes wonder what sort of person I'd be if life had been easy, without hard times and without my faith constantly challenged. Not having to admit I'm not in control, but God is and He has a plan for our lives surpassing all imagination.

When faced with the thought most cancer patients immediately have, "Why me?" the best answer I know is, "Why not me?" I cannot change yesterday or control tomorrow. I want to live in the moment, understand God has a purpose for my breast cancer, and seize every chance I get to share a smile with someone.

> ***And God is faithful; He will not let you be tempted***
> ***beyond what you can bear. But when you are***
> ***temped, He will provide a way out, so that you can stand up under it.***
> ***—-1 Corinthians 10:13***

ABOUT THE AUTHOR

My name is Juanita Vianelle. I have been with my husband David, my best friend since we were 13 and 15. We will celebrate our 57-year anniversary February 12, 2023. Raised three children son Eric, daughter Kimberly, and son Michael. I was my grandfather's birthday gift and my granddaughter, Alexandra, was mine.

Born in Texas and moved to California when I was three. Lived in Gilroy 1966-1996. Moved to Bend Oregon 1996-2014. Live in Beaverton, Oregon 2014 to present.

Dental Technician for many years, but a stay-at-home mom for twelve. Quit dental field to open a preschool for my last 10 years in California and taught piano.

While in Bend for 19 years, I enjoyed many of the outdoor activities, especially during winter. Leaving my large gardens where I spent much of my home time, I am now grateful for our condominium lifestyle. A deck garden with very few to zero weeds. Many walking trails and a small lake nearby to walk my dog, Daisy.

One of my favorite things to have spent years doing was volunteering at St. Charles Hospital in Bend and St. Vincent Hospital in Portland until Covid shutdown the volunteer department. Now I am busy with Daisy, writing, baking, trying new dinner recipes, finding new walking trails, and convincing myself to get back into Tai Chi instead of being hooked on Netflix K-dramas series since the start of Covid.

My wish is for the world to be like a snow globe. When troubled times come, one shake and everything becomes surreal.

www.ingramcontent.com/pod-product-compliance
Lightning Source LLC
Chambersburg PA
CBHW060403080526
44583CB00012B/446